THE BEST IS NOW!

Delight yourself in the Lord and He shall give you the desires of your heart.

Ps. 37:4

Esther Herriott

THE BEST IS NOW!

Learning to Love Every Stage of Life

Esther M. Herriott

To my precious friend, Michelle: Life is precious & special & worth the joy: let's work on this for a more stress free life: Love Donna

iUniverse, Inc.
New York Lincoln Shanghai

The Best is Now!
Learning to Love Every Stage of Life

iUniverse books may be ordered through booksellers or by contacting:

iUniverse
2021 Pine Lake Road, Suite 100
Lincoln, NE 68512
www.iuniverse.com
1-800-Authors (1-800-288-4677)

ISBN: 978-0-595-45594-2 (pbk)
ISBN: 978-0-595-89895-4 (ebk)

Printed in the United States of America

CONTENTS

INTRODUCTION

Do you love going on trips? I do. Long ones, short ones, pleasant ones, even hectic ones, I enjoy them all. The thought occurred to me that life is like a long trip and it's up to us to make it as enjoyable as possible. I was more than halfway through my life's journey before I found the secret to make it enjoyable.

I have met many women who are not enjoying their present age whether it be thirty, forty, fifty or above because they can't help thinking about what their life will be like as they get older. I've heard comments such as, "I was so depressed the day I turned forty." Or, "I dread the day I become fifty." That's what prompted me to write this book. I would like to encourage women to enjoy whatever stage of life they are in. For those who are concerned about aging, I know from my own experience that life can have productive, fulfilling years at every age. One may be a little different from the other, but they are all full of exciting opportunities.

Robert Browning said, *"Grow old with me, the best is yet to come."* Although it's good to be optimistic about our future, it's even better to start enjoying today by believing, THE BEST IS NOW!

CHAPTER 1

▼

FEELING LOVED

The most important thing in a woman's life is feeling loved. From infancy to old age we long to be loved. We're good at giving love, but most of us don't receive it as often as we would like. We know that God loves us, but sometimes that isn't enough. We want to feel loved by someone who can hug us and tell us we're loved. Whether it is a husband, boyfriend, parent, sibling, child or friend, we want and need to know they love us.

Growing up I was a chubby child with red, curly hair and way too many freckles. How I hated red hair and freckles. But most of all I hated being chubby. I wasn't obese, but when we shopped for dresses I had to buy the ones labeled "chubby." I've disliked that word ever since. In seventh grade I was not only a little overweight, but I was 5'7" and wore Buster Brown winged-tipped shoes size 8 ½. Can't you just picture that? If you recall seventh grade you may remember the boys were mostly about 4'10", so I was nine inches taller. Like most seventh grade girls I wanted boys to be attracted to me, but most of them just teased me about my red hair, freckles, my height and weight. I can still hear their taunts, "Fatty, Fatty two-by-four, can't get through the kitchen door." Then there were other little rhymes about red hair that were even worse. Some kids can be unkind!

There was another redheaded girl in my class who was also tall and had freckles, but she was slender and beautiful, and she wore very classy-looking clothes. She also wore makeup (which I was forbidden to do) and her hair was very stylish. I envied her because the boys were all crazy about her. Many days I went home in tears feeling like the "ugly duckling." When my mother noticed I had been crying she could always get me to tell her what was wrong. Then she would give me a big hug and say, "I think you're beautiful and I love you." I'm sure she really meant it, but mothers all think their children are beautiful. Even though I didn't believe her, I always felt better afterwards. Isn't it interesting how much better we feel when someone gives us a hug and says, "I love you"?

DATE WITH THE KING

The year I started high school my family moved from a small town in upstate New York to Waxahachie, Texas, a small town just south of Dallas. Once I got over being angry about leaving my friends I gradually began to enjoy my new school. I was sort of popular, but mostly among the girls. Boys liked me in a sisterly way, not as someone they wanted to date. I was still 5'7" but by now the boys were taller so I didn't tower over them. I no longer wore the ugly Buster Browns and my red hair, which I hated in junior high, was now long and beautiful, my best feature. I didn't have to feel envious of other people's pretty clothes because we all wore uniforms. Navy blue dresses with long sleeves, hems thirteen inches from the floor, and white starched collars and cuffs. (I'll bet you're laughing!) However, I was still a little plump. One day I overheard some boys talking about me saying, "She would really be a knockout if she'd lose about twenty pounds." Oh, that hurt! But instead of determining I would lose weight, I went home and drowned my sorrows with some soft white bread slathered with peanut butter and honey. Food was my comfort.

In my senior year our school held a banquet (in lieu of a prom since it was a Christian school which frowned upon dancing). The students elected a king and queen. I don't recall who was chosen as queen, but I definitely remember the tall, handsome blonde who became king. His name was Jim Hicks. I nearly fainted when he asked me to be his date for the banquet. I was so excited I could hardly wait to get home to tell my mother. She looked sad as she told me they could not afford to pay for my ticket or buy me a new dress or shoes to wear to the banquet. I was devastated! Even if I could come up with the money to buy the ticket, how could I go without something new to wear? The ugly navy blue uniforms with white starched collars and cuffs just wouldn't cut it for a date with Jim Hicks, the tall, blonde, handsome king.

When Mother saw how upset I was she lovingly suggested we pray about it. So we did, and God answered our prayer. My older brother, Bob, who was in the Army, sent a check to buy material for mother to make me a new dress and buy some shoes. He even sent me a string of pearls. And then, God provided an anonymous person to pay for my banquet ticket. God is so good! The night of the banquet I felt like a queen as I walked arm in arm with Jim proudly wearing my new pale blue dress, black patent leather shoes and a beautiful pink corsage. I really felt loved. Loved by God for answering my prayer, loved by my mother for making my dress, loved by my brother for sending money and also by Jim, the king, for choosing me to be his date. Feeling loved is a wonderful thing!

LOOKING FOR LOVE

As a teenager I recall that most of the girls had marriage on their minds. I was one of those. Since childhood I had dreamed of the day I would walk down a church aisle in a poofy white wedding dress. I was sure that getting married would make me happy because I would have someone besides my parents to love me. Proverbs 19:22 says *"What a man desires is unfailing love."* (NIV) We all want that unfailing love and we expect to find it when we get married, however, marriage doesn't always meet our expectations. Six days after my nineteenth birthday I had a lovely wedding wearing an elegant white satin dress with tiny buttons all the way down the back and a long veil adorned with lilies of the valley across the headpiece. I felt so beautiful. I was sure my dreams had come true at last. But then came the marriage! Sometimes weddings and marriages are two different things. My marriage was far from what I expected. I definitely didn't find the kind of love I had been longing for.

I went through two divorces searching for that unfailing love the Bible talks about in Proverbs. Finally at the age of forty-eight I met and married my third husband, Jud. This time I was sure I had found the man who would make me happy.... who would give me the kind of love I had always desired.

A SATISFYING LOVE

After a few months of marriage to Jud I realized there was something missing in our marriage. I didn't feel loved by Jud the way I had expected to even though he was a wonderful husband. I didn't understand why I wasn't happy. I was embarrassed to tell him how I felt, so I started praying about it. As I prayed I sensed that God understood my need to feel loved. He was not condemning with me, He was loving and gentle. He helped me understand that I was expecting more from Jud than he was able to give.... that only God could satisfy this craving for love that was within me. It made me aware that I didn't really have a close relationship with God. How could I expect Him to make me feel loved? This prompted me to start reading my Bible and spending time in prayer. Gradually I began to develop a deeper relationship with God and before long I noticed I was feeling happier. I didn't have that unfulfilled longing for love anymore. Jud hadn't changed, but I had. God's love was making me feel like a whole person and I became contented with my marriage and my life. I like the wording of Ephesians 5:2 in *THE MES-SAGE*. "*Mostly what God does is love you. Keep company with him and learn a life of love. Observe how Christ loved us. His love was not cautious but extravagant. He didn't love in order to get something from us but to give everything of himself to us.*"

A LOVING FATHER

For those of you who grew up with a father who showed you affection and told you he loved you, you can probably relate to God as a loving Father. If you had a father who was gone most of the time, was an alcoholic, abusive, or simply did not know how to show his love, it may take you quite a while to fully understand that God is a loving Father who wants to make you feel loved. There could also be other reasons why we may have a difficult time relating to God as a loving father. One of them is rejection. Many of us have experienced rejection by teachers, classmates, boyfriends, people in our church or family members. Rejection can cause us to have such low self-esteem that we don't think anyone could love us, not even God.

When I was about six years old I visited my cousins, Kenny, June and Nancy, in Long Island, New York. One night the three of us were all sitting on the steps together just before bedtime when my Uncle Russell came over to the stairway to give his children a good-night-kiss. I thought, "Oh how I wish my father was like that." Then Uncle Russell asked me, "Would you like a kiss too?" A little embarrassed, I shyly replied, "Yes." I've always remembered Uncle Russell's sweet kiss. He was so gentle and loving. I had never had this kind of affection shown to me by my father. I'm sure my father loved me, but he seldom had time for me. Because of this it was many years before I was able to picture God as a Father who wanted to shower me with love. When I was finally able to believe He was a loving God who wanted me to be happy, it made a huge difference in my relationship with God as well as my husband.

GIVING LOVE

Receiving love is important to all of us, but giving love is also important. When I think of giving love the first thing that comes to mind is the overwhelming love I experienced when I held each of my three precious daughters in my arms for the first time. You women who have experienced giving birth know exactly what I am talking about. The love you feel the moment the nurse puts that tiny baby into your arms is simply indescribable. As a young girl I had always dreamed of the day I would have babies of my own, but I never knew it would be so wonderful. I was blessed with three beautiful redheaded daughters, Deborah, Barbara and Rebecca. Nothing could have been more perfect. I grew up with four brothers, no sisters, so I was thrilled to have daughters, especially redheaded ones. Whenever I would hear people say that God loves us more than we love our children, I couldn't comprehend it because I felt such a strong love for my three girls. I wanted them to feel loved by me.

It's easy to give love to our children or our loved ones (most of them anyway), but how easy is it to give love to people we consider unlovable? In the natural it's not something we can do, but with God's help we can. If we could put ourselves into someone else's shoes so we know what makes them tick, I am sure we would not find them so unlovable. I have found that praying for people who I find difficult to love changes my feelings toward them. When I begin praying for them God gives me compassion and understanding for them and little by little I discover they're not really so bad. In fact I might even want to be friends with them. Giving love is just as important as receiving love because God tells us to do it. I John 3:11 says, "*We should love one another.*" (NIV) It doesn't say, "We should love those who are nice to us and say good things about us." "One another" includes everyone. Whenever I have thought, "It's impossible to love them, Lord." I just ask Him to help me love them. It's amazing how He can change our feelings when we're open to it.

LOVE PATS

Have you ever heard the term "love pats?" When I was a child my parents would give me a pat on the head and when I would ask, "What was that for?" they'd tell me, "That's a love pat." Since then when something happens that makes me feel especially loved, I call it a "love pat." I took a survey asking women, "What makes you feel loved?" The two leading answers were: "people spending time with me and listening to me." Whether it's our husbands, our children, our parents or our friends, having them spend time with us, really listening to what we say, means a great deal to us. Yes, I would definitely call that a "love pat."

What are some "love pats" you enjoy remembering? Try making a list and it may surprise you how many you can think of.

List of "Love Pats"

_____

_____

Some "love pats" that come to my mind are things like:

- A high tea given by a dear friend to celebrate my sixtieth birthday.

- Receiving a letter from my ten-year-old when she was at camp.

- Hearing my grandbaby say for the first time, "I wuv you, Meemaw."

- Receiving a call from either of my two daughters who live in this area inviting me to go shopping or to a movie.

- Receiving a bouquet of flowers on Mother's Day from my youngest daughter who lives in Texas.

A very memorable "love pat" was when I skidded on an icy road and my car spun in a complete circle putting me right into the path of an oncoming car. Just before we collided it spun again all the way to the other side of the road. I expected to end up in the nearby field, but suddenly it was as though someone picked up my car, turned it around, and placed it back on the road heading in the right direction. I went on my way crying and thanking God all the way home. I really believe God sent an angel, or maybe two, to protect me from what could have been a terrible accident. The Bible says in Psalm 91:11 *"For He will command his angels concerning you to guard you in all your ways. (NIV)* I felt very loved by God that day.

Do you ever experience a warm feeling all over your body while you're praying? (I'm not talking about hot flashes!) When that happens to me I know it's a "love pat" from God. It makes me feel like God is right there in the room giving me a big hug and whispering in my ear, "I love you."

THE PERFECT KIND OF LOVE

When God shows us His love in various ways, it reassures us that He loves us. We gradually start believing that it is possible for Him to satisfy our loneliness, make us feel good about ourselves, heal the memories that make our hearts ache, or replace anxiety with peace. His love is unconditional, it will never hurt us, never disappoint us. Even if we turn away from Him for a time, like some of us have done, He will continue to love us and will always be waiting for us to return to Him. He doesn't care if we are twenty years old or sixty, if our hair is golden blonde or snowy white. It doesn't matter if we have a beautiful, slender body or if we're a little overweight. He doesn't look at our outward appearance, He looks at our hearts. Whether we have made terrible mistakes in our past, or we have always been model Christians, He loves all of us the same.... there are no favorites. God simply wants to shower us with His love and have us love Him in return.

A GIFT OF GRACE

God is a God of grace. I call my wonderful husband, Jud, my gift of grace. We've all heard it said that grace is unmerited favor ... a gift we receive even though we don't deserve it. That's the way I feel about Jud. He is a serious Melancholy personality so he isn't a "fun" person, he isn't very romantic, not too affectionate, but he makes me feel very loved. Let me tell you why.

He does so many nice things for me unnoticed like getting my car washed and filling it with gas, balancing my checkbook and keeping money in my bank account, emptying all the wastebaskets, recording programs on TV that I enjoy, polishing the counters in the kitchen and bathroom, going to the Post Office and cleaners, helping clean up the kitchen after dinner, slipping money into my wallet,.... and these are just a few of the nice things he does. He is very generous and loving to my daughters and grandchildren. He bought a timeshare in Branson, Missouri so we could get away together for fun times. He encourages and supports me in everything I attempt to do. He gives me good advice when I ask for it, but doesn't try to tell me what to do when I don't ask for it. Most of all he has become the spiritual leader of our home. I think that's what every Christian woman longs for. It isn't hard to be submissive to a husband who listens to the voice of the Lord. When the Bible says a husband should love his wife as Christ loved the Church, Jud comes as close as anyone I know. Now you know why I call him my gift of grace and why I feel very loved.

WHAT'S AHEAD?

When you celebrate a birthday entering a new decade, what kind of thoughts go through your head? Do you enjoy your day? Are you happy about your age and what's going on in your life? Are you anticipating the year ahead excited about what it holds in store? Are you full of confidence and hope? If not, ask yourself, "Why not?" There are times when all of us don't especially like some of the physical changes we feel in our bodies or see reflected in our mirrors. We may allow negative thoughts to fill our minds, such as, "I'm unattractive, incompetent and hopeless? I don't feel loved." Then we allow ourselves to have a pity party.... we get depressed. As women we all want to feel loved, beautiful and useful. If only we could understand how much God loves us and how beautiful we are in His eyes, it might prevent us from having those "down days". When we read God's Word we see that He has good plans for us, so we don't need to worry about the changes that take place in us as we grow older. Our looks may change a little and we may not be able to do some of the things we did in our twenties, but whatever our age, God will always open new doors of opportunity for us. We can rest assured that there will be exciting, rewarding years ahead.

My purpose in writing this book is to encourage each of you to enjoy life wherever you are along your journey. In the chapters ahead I will share with you how God has brought me through some difficult years to the place I am today. He has shown me ways to prepare for my older years so they will be enjoyable. Although I am getting older, I can say with all my heart, "THE BEST IS NOW!"

CHAPTER 2

▼

WHAT'S MY DESTINY?

As a child I loved coloring books about movie stars so I could color all their pretty clothes. In my junior high years I liked to draw fancy dresses thinking that one day I might be a dress designer. Then in high school I was sure I would be a missionary to South America because my Spanish teacher, a former missionary, told exciting stories of her ministry in Argentina. Being a Christian high school, there were a number of guys planning to enter the ministry, so I began thinking maybe I was meant to be a preacher's wife. I can't say that these were God's thoughts, they were just the imaginings of a young girl. As it turned out, I did none of these things. I know God had a destiny for me, but I'm sorry to say it took me over fifty years to discover it.

Maybe some of you are like me, slow in finding God's plan for your life. Perhaps you still haven't discovered your destiny. It's such a comfort to know that when we miss it, God doesn't say, "Too bad. You missed your chance. I have no use for you now." Fortunately God is not like that. He's a God of second chances, or more if we need them.

If we were destined to be Olympic figure skaters but were unwilling to devote the necessary time to train for it until we were forty-five, chances are unlikely we'd make it to the Olympics. But that's okay. God has something else that's perfectly suited to our age and circumstances.

NOW WHAT?

After we have passed the seasons of college, marriage, raising children, and have entered into the empty-nest period, some of us may wonder, "Now what? Is life going to be boring and empty from now on?" No, no, no! There's so much more! The word destiny means "a predetermined course of events." These events are all planned ahead of time by God. In the Bible the Apostle Paul wrote, *"we are pre-destined according to the purpose of Him who works all things according to the counsel of His will,"*(Ephesians 1:11) and in 2:10 *he says, "For we are God's workmanship, created in Christ Jesus to do good works, which God prepared in advance for us to do."* (NIV) So you see, God had a purpose for us even before we were born. That purpose was not to retire from life at age forty, fifty, or sixty.... maybe not even seventy. There are many opportunities available to us if we are willing to take advantage of them. When we know we are fulfilling our destiny life becomes exciting and happy.

Do you ever ask yourself, "If God has a plan for me, what is it?" It's easy to think we are following God's plan when everything in our lives is going smoothly, but when we encounter some difficult times, we're quick to think we may have missed His plan altogether. Let's take a look at some of the people in the Bible who could have felt they missed God's plan, but instead they had complete faith in His providence.

GOD'S PLAN FOR QUEEN ESTHER

Esther was a young Jewish girl whose parents were killed when she was just a child. She was raised by a loving older cousin named Mordecai. When the king of Persia was in search of a wife, many beautiful, virgin women were brought to the palace to be presented to the king. Esther was taken, probably against her will, to be one of these women. Of all the women who were brought before the king, Esther was the one he chose to be his wife, the new Queen of Persia. The Bible says he loved Esther more than all the women. Don't you love stories like this where a poor young girl becomes a beautiful queen and lives in a palace for the rest of her life? It sounds like a fairy tale but it was God's destiny for Esther.

Not everything was a bed of roses for Esther after she became queen. An evil man named Haman, who had a very important position in the palace, had a deep hatred for the Jewish people living in Persia. He came up with a plot to have them all destroyed and was able to convince the king it would be in his best interest to get rid of all Jews. When Esther heard about this plot she knew the time had come to divulge the secret she had kept from her husband, that she was a

Jew. Her uncle reminded her that perhaps God had put her in the palace *"for such a time as this."* She knew she must do whatever she could to save her people from being destroyed. At that time there was a law prohibiting anyone from entering into the king's presence without an invitation from him, under penalty of death. This law even applied to Esther, so she knew she would be risking her life to walk into his chambers without permission, She could have felt that she totally missed God's plan for her life, that her life was over along with all the Jewish people residing in Persia, but she had a strong faith in God that He would deliver her people, so she bravely entered the king's throne room without permission. When the king saw Esther, he lowered his scepter, which meant she was welcome to enter. He said, *"What do you wish, Queen Esther? What is your request? It shall be given to you—up to half the kingdom!"* I like to think his heart melted at the sight of her because he loved her. Don't you imagine that Esther breathed a big sigh of relief when he beckoned her to come in? If you have never read the book of Esther in the Bible, I would highly recommend it. It's a beautiful story with a happy ending. The Jews' lives were spared and Esther's loving uncle was appointed to a position of high authority in the king's palace in place of the wicked Haman. Esther was able to continue reigning as the Queen of Persia. The name of God is never mentioned in this book, but it is a good example of God's destiny for Esther as well as the Jewish people.

GOD'S PLAN FOR MOSES

Moses' mother must have believed God had a special destiny for her son. When Moses was born the Hebrews were slaves in Egypt and Pharaoh was afraid of them because he thought they might take over his country. He ordered that all Hebrew baby boys be killed at birth so they would not grow up and fight against him. To save Moses' life his mother put him into a homemade basket and placed it among the reeds along the side of the River Nile. Moses' sister Miriam watched over him until Pharaoh's daughter came to the river to wash one morning and her maids found Moses in his basket. When the Pharaoh's daughter saw him she loved him immediately because he was such a beautiful baby, so he was taken to the palace and raised as her own son.

This sounds as though God had a plan for Moses, doesn't it? But years later when Moses killed an Egyptian who was mistreating one of the Jews, he knew he could be put to death so he had to flee for his life. Do you suppose he missed God's plan? It might sound that way to us because the Bible doesn't tell us much about him for the next forty years except that he was a shepherd in a desert area. But then at the age of eighty God asked him to return to Egypt. By this time a new pharaoh was reigning in Egypt who probably didn't know about Moses killing a man, so he didn't have to fear for his life. God asked Moses to go before the pharaoh and tell him that God said to let His people go. In the first five books of the Old Testament Moses tells how God's plan unfolded. The pharaoh finally consented to let the Israelites leave Egypt, but it took forty years traveling through the hot desert before they finally reached the promised land of Canaan. His life story ends on Mount Nebo where Moses died at the age of 120. In Deuteronomy 34:7 it says, "*Moses was a hundred and twenty years old when he died, yet his eyes were not weak nor his strength gone.*" Even though he may have encountered detours along the way, we can see that God had a plan for Moses from his birth to his death. What a beautiful picture. It not only encourages us that God has a plan for us, but that He can still use us to accomplish great things in our older years.

GOD'S PLAN FOR JOSEPH

Joseph's father, Jacob, had twelve sons but the two youngest ones were born from his true love, Rachel. Because of his deep love for Rachel he was partial to Joseph and his brother Benjamin. Joseph became his favorite and to show his love Jacob made him a beautiful coat which was usually given to the oldest son. This caused his ten older brothers to become jealous of him and they began to hate him. When Joseph was seventeen years old he had two dreams in which his brothers were bowing down to him. He foolishly shared his dreams with his brothers who became very angry. One day Joseph's father asked him to go check on his brothers who were tending their flocks in fields quite a distance from home. When they saw him approaching wearing his beautiful coat Jacob had made for him their jealousy rose up in them. They plotted together to kill him. They grabbed him and threw him into a pit. But one brother wanted to spare his life so he talked them into selling Joseph to some slave traders who were passing by on their way to Egypt. They took off his beautiful coat and dipped it in the blood of an animal, then took it to their father telling him that Joseph had been killed by wild animals. If this had happened to you, do you think you would have questioned God about this being your destiny? Read on!

Joseph was taken to Egypt where he was sold to Potiphar, an officer of the pharaoh of Egypt. He didn't allow himself to have a pity party. Instead he did his best to be a good servant. His good conduct earned him the highest position in the household. Joseph was a handsome man and Potiphar's wife was attracted to him. She tried to seduce him but when he rejected her she accused him of raping her which resulted in Joseph being thrown into prison. Instead of being angry, insisting he was innocent, Joseph became a model prisoner. His good conduct earned him a position of responsibility over the other prisoners.

Two years went by and Joseph was still in prison. But one night the pharaoh had a dream which no one could interpret. Someone told Pharaoh that Joseph had accurately interpreted dreams for two prisoners, so he sent for Joseph to see if he could interpret his dream. Joseph told him that there would be seven years of good harvests in Egypt followed by seven years of famine. He explained to Pharaoh that they should store corn so they would not starve. Because God showed Joseph the interpretation, the pharaoh said, *"inasmuch as God has shown you all this, there is no one as discerning and wise as you. You shall be over my house, and all my people shall be ruled according to your word; only in regard to the throne will I be greater than you."* The king was so grateful to Joseph he gave him his signet ring making him the second most influential man in all of Egypt. He was also appointed as Food Commissioner, so no one could purchase food without Joseph's consent.

When it came to pass that there was a famine in Canaan, Joseph's brothers came to Egypt to purchase grain. Since Joseph was the Food Commissioner they had to come to him. As they knelt before Joseph seeking permission to buy grain, he remembered the dream he had about his brothers bowing down to him. It's a touching story how Joseph forgave his brothers and their whole family was reconciled. Joseph fulfilled God's destiny for him even though he experienced some very difficult times.

GOD'S PLAN FOR NAOMI

Many of us have heard about Ruth in the Bible, but perhaps not her mother-in-law, Naomi. Naomi was a Jew living in Bethlehem with her husband and two sons until a severe famine led them to go to the country of Moab in search of food. This might be like my moving to Iraq where I would live among Muslins rather than Christians. It must have been difficult for her. While they were there Naomi's husband died and not long afterward both sons also died. Naomi was devastated and she became very bitter.

When the famine in her homeland came to an end Naomi decided to return home. It was very depressing for her to return home without a husband or children. She told her two daughters-in-law they should remain in Moab where they would undoubtedly be able to remarry. However, one of them, Ruth, insisted on accompanying Naomi back to Bethlehem. She loved her mother-in-law and was committed to caring for her.

This was the beginning of happier days for Naomi. Not long after they returned to Bethlehem Ruth married a wealthy relative of Naomi's and gave birth to a son (who later became the grandfather to King David). Any of us who are mothers or grandmothers can appreciate how happy Naomi must have been to be able to have a grandson to love. It brings tears to my eyes whenever I read Ruth 4:14-16: *"Then the women said to Naomi, 'Blessed be the LORD, who has not left you this day without a near kinsman; and may his name be famous in Israel! And may he be to you a restorer of life and a nourisher of your old age; for your daughter-in-law, who loves you, who it better to you than seven sons, has borne him.' Then Naomi took the child and laid him on her bosom, and became a nurse to him."* For centuries God has used this story of Naomi to encourage women that God has a plan for each of us. We have a destiny!

GOD'S PLAN FOR US

I enjoy working jigsaw puzzles. Recently when I was working on a puzzle the thought occurred to me that our lives are like a puzzle all laid out on a table in front of God. He knows which ones are the edge pieces,(the most important ones) and He also knows there are no missing pieces. Although He puts in one piece at a time, He sees the finished product from the very beginning. He's aware that for some of us it may take quite a while to complete the whole picture. If we really believe that God has a plan for us all the way to the end of our lives, it will make it easier for us to go through the difficult times without giving up hope. In Jeremiah 29:11 God told the Israelites, *"For I know the plans I have for you,"* declares the LORD, *"plans to prosper you and not to harm you, plans to give you hope and a future."* This verse wasn't only for people in Bible times, it applies to us as well. God has good plans for us and He gives us hope for whatever is ahead.

Sometimes things happen to us that may not be part of God's plan, but He can use them to build character in us. I had a bad experience when I was twelve years old which left me with hatred in my heart towards someone for nearly forty years. When we harbor bitterness inside us we don't realize the effect it has on us, as well as those around us. It affects many of the decisions we make in our lives, the way we relate to people, and sometimes it even has an adverse effect on our health. I was in my fifties before I became aware I had never forgiven this person. God impressed upon me the need to forgive. I could not ignore the scripture verse that says, *"For if you forgive men when they sin against you, your heavenly Father will also forgive you. But if you do not forgive men their sins, your Father will not forgive your sins.* (Matthew 6:14-15 (NIV) God knew I could not do this on my own so He already had it planned for me to attend a seminar at a friend's church. Wouldn't you know it was about forgiveness? I learned how God can help us forgive anyone, no matter what they have done. Once I was able to forgive this person I felt a great sense of freedom. No more hatred or bitterness. Since that time God has allowed me to use that experience to help other people who are harboring unforgiveness in their lives.

SHAPING OUR LIVES

Have you ever watched a potter forming a vase on his rapidly-spinning wheel? He takes a big lump of clay and centers it on the wheel, then shapes it with his hands as it spins around. If it gets off center he has to firmly pull it back or it will be misshapen, it won't be the beautiful vase he had in mind. This is a good analogy of our lives. In the Bible the prophet Isaiah likens us to a piece of clay. "ISA 64:8 *"Yet, O LORD, you are our Father. We are the clay, you are the potter; we are all the work of your hand."* (NIV) We're that clay on the wheel and we get off center.... not following God's plan.... so He tries to pull us back. He knows what He has in mind for us, but if we don't stay in the center of the wheel with His hands firmly around us, we won't turn out to be what He has planned for our lives.

After the potter finishes shaping the vase he puts it into a blazing hot oven. This is necessary to make the vase strong so it won't fall apart. The Psalmist David said in Psalm 12:6 *"We are like silver refined in a furnace of clay, purified seven times."* (NIV) I'm sure all of us have had times in our lives when we felt as though we were inside that hot oven. It was painful and we didn't think we could stand the heat, but later we realized the heat made us stronger and more able to cope with life's difficulties. I'm sure none of us want to be a vase with cracks in it. We would be useless! We wouldn't be able to hold a beautiful bouquet of roses because all the water would leak out. God's plan for us is to be useful as well as beautiful.

LIFE IS SHORT

Have you ever thought about how short life is? The older we get, the more we think about it. Many of us wonder if we have fulfilled our destinies. Have we been or done whatever God had planned for us? In the Bible King David said *"Human life is like grass; we grow like a flower in the field. After the wind blows, the flower is gone, and there is no sign of where it was."* Psalm 103:15-16 (NCV) What are we doing with our lives? Are we satisfied that we are following God's plan?

When God created Adam and Eve He had a wonderful plan for them, but they messed up.... ruined the plan. God created all of us with freedom of choice and Adam and Eve chose to disobey by eating that forbidden fruit. God knew ahead of time that they would mess up but He still loved them and had a plan for their lives. It's the same with us. He knows everything we're going to do before we ever do it. Even if we don't follow His plan, He still loves us and continually tries to bring us back to the original plan He had for our lives. We will never feel contented or fulfilled living outside of God's plan.

FOLLOW YOUR DREAMS

What are some of the things you would like to do with your life? Many of us have dreams we haven't pursued. Is that true of you? You may wonder if your dreams are the plans God has in mind for you. If you are not sure, unless they are totally contrary to God's Word, why not give it a try? Some choices you might consider could require special education so you may have to go back to school. Nothing wrong with that! I took a couple of college classes when I was in my fifties, and after I got used to being the oldest person in the class I enjoyed them very much. Lots of women pursue their education after their children leave home. Some women start businesses in their homes so they can be with their young children or a handicapped loved one. Grandma Moses followed her dream and became a famous artist at the age of eighty. Think about it … maybe it's not too late to follow your dream.

PRO 19:21 *"Many are the plans in a man's heart, but it is the LORD'S purpose that prevails."* (NIV) If you really desire to follow God's plan for your life, just ask Him to show you what it is. I sensed God wanted me to be a women's speaker many years before I had the opportunity to actually speak so I began preparing for it. I attended classes, read books, and listened to tapes about speaking. Finally the day came when I began to receive speaking invitations. I was thrilled. I was following my dream. The same was true with writing. I thought God wanted me to share some of my experiences with other women by writing magazine articles and now a book, so I've taken writing classes and read many books on the subject. I've had more rejections than acceptances but I'm still writing. I spent two years writing this book, then after being critiqued I rewrote the whole thing. It's been a learning experience but I've enjoyed it. Someone once said, "Some people see things and say, 'Why?' I dream of things that never were and say, 'Why not?'" Be bold! Follow your dreams.

Florence Littauer tells a story of her mother-in-law who always desired to be an opera singer, but her parents insisted she work in the family business. When she became elderly, afflicted with Alzheimer's disease, although she talked to no one, she was often heard singing opera. As Florence puts it, "She died with the dream still inside her." Don't let that happen to you.

What are your dreams? If you have always felt that God had a plan for your life which has never materialized, don't give up. Perhaps now is the time to pursue it. Remember, God had your life all planned before you were born. He's ready and willing to help you fulfill your destiny.

CHAPTER 3

▼

TIRED OF BEING SHALLOW!

I was one of those busy Christian ladies who took their children to everything the church offered, taught Sunday School, sang in the choir, knitted pom-pom slippers for the missionaries, headed up rummage and bake sales, attended Bible studies.... I did it all. But I was shallow! If you had told me so at that time I would have denied it. But now, in retrospect I know it's true. I had invited Jesus into my life as a young girl so I considered myself a Christian. I was confident I would go to heaven when I died, but I didn't realize there was much more God had planned for me to make my life complete.

As young women we think our lives will be perfect once we have that fabulous wedding and marry that handsome man. Then we think children will bring us the satisfaction we desire. We spend many years living for our husbands and children, then our nest is empty. What then? Some of us go to college to finish our education which was interrupted when we chose to get married. Some of us embark on the career we always wanted. Getting married, having children, completing our education, starting a career ... all of these things are good, but quite often we find there's still a void that hasn't been filled. Are you one of those women who is searching for something more? If so, God has more for you. He wants to lead you on a spiritual journey that will be more satisfying than anything you have ever experienced.

GETTING TO KNOW GOD

I believe that deep within all of us is a desire to know God, and God has a desire to know us. Inside each one of us is a spirit. Our bodies will die eventually but our spirits will go on living forever. Our spirit is the part of us that has a relationship with God. The only way to satisfy that longing inside us is to allow God to come into our lives and make our spirit one with His. You may be asking, "How can God's Spirit be one with my spirit?" Most people say they believe in God and many say they believe the Bible is the inspired Word of God, but when you ask them if they have a personal relationship with God they don't know what that is. The Bible states if we love God we will also love His Son, Jesus Christ. By believing what the Bible says about Jesus being God's Son, that He died on a cross so we could be forgiven of our sin, that He was buried in a tomb, then arose from the dead three days later and now lives in heaven.... if we believe all this we can invite Jesus into our lives. Once we do this God's Spirit enters into us making our spirit one with His. From that moment on He is always with us wherever we go, whatever we do.

It's God's desire for each of us to be part of His family ... to know that He is our Father. This is an important part of the journey we're taking with God. If you have never invited Jesus into your life, this chapter may not make much sense to you, but if you have a desire in your heart to be a child of God I invite you to do so right now before you read any further. The Bible says that all of us have sinned, no matter how good we are, so we must ask God to forgive us and invite Jesus into our hearts if we want to know without a doubt that we will spend eternity in heaven with Him. Our spirits are going to live forever, either in heaven or a place separated from God, so this is your opportunity to make a choice where you will spend eternity. If you would like to accept Jesus into your heart, here is a simple prayer to pray, or you can use your own words, whichever is more comfortable for you.

Dear Jesus,

I know that I am a sinner and need your forgiveness. I believe You are the Son of God and You died for my sins. Today I choose to turn away from my sin and I now invite You to come into my heart. I want to live a life that's pleasing to You from this day forward.

In Jesus' Name, Amen.

If you just prayed this prayer, the angels in heaven are rejoicing. Your name is now written in God's Book of Life and you can know for certain that when you leave this earth you will live forever in heaven.

Some people never know who their natural fathers are. This leaves them with a sadness all their lives. We don't have to wonder who our spiritual Father is. We can know without a doubt. *"Yet to all who received him, to those who believed in his name, he gave the right to become children of God."* John 1:12 (NIV) When God is our Father and we are His children His Spirit will always be inside us guiding us and making us feel loved and valued.

ADOPTED CHILDREN

Once we have accepted Jesus as our Savior we are adopted into God's family. God is our Father; we are His children. We are heirs to God, which entitles us to everything God owns. What an awesome thought! *"in love he predestined us to be adopted as his sons through Jesus Christ, in accordance with his pleasure and will."* Ephesians 1:4-5 (NIV) I remember the day my daughter, Barbara, and her husband, Gary, adopted a beautiful baby boy with big dimples and dark brown eyes and hair. Because they were unable to have children during their twelve years of marriage, they had often talked about adoption, but Barb wanted to have her own baby. In prayer one day she cried out to God with tears streaming down her face, "God, I want to have a baby who looks like us, who has our characteristics, our DNA." Immediately she sensed God telling her, "I adopted you, but you didn't look like me or have my blood. I adopted you because I chose you to be mine, and then I gave you my spirit of adoption, my blood, my DNA." He convinced her that she didn't have to be afraid about adopting a child that wasn't part of her. From that moment on she started praying about it, and soon she began to have a desire to adopt a baby. When they received a phone call advising them there was a baby available for them they were both overjoyed.

The day they went to court to sign the adoption papers for their three-day-old son, they were able to meet the baby's birth mother, a seventeen-year-old girl, and her mother. It was thrilling for Barb and Gary to see that the baby's mother resembled Gary so much she could have easily passed for his sister. It was a very emotional time as the mother and grandmother said goodbye to their tiny baby boy.

As Barb and Gary read through the document to be signed, they were touched as they read, "For all intents and purposes of inheritance it shall be just as if Luke Ephraim Schmitz was born to Barbara Ann Schmitz." They had not realized how permanent adoption is. Everything they owned would one day rightfully be his and no one could take their baby away from them. Luke would forever be their child, their heir.

That's how it is with us. God has adopted us. No one can take us away from Him. We are going to share in his inheritance; it's irrevocable. Think of it! Not only are we His children forever for Him to love, protect, and provide for, but we are heirs to God, entitled to everything that belongs to Him.

WHEN I BECAME GOD'S CHILD

I became God's child when I was just a young girl living in Geneva, New York where my father was pastor of a small church. We lived in an apartment above the church which was located in a storefront on a busy downtown street. In addition to the hall used for a sanctuary there was an office for my father and a gymnasium where my brothers and I liked to play. Our backyard was a tarpaper roof above the gymnasium where Mother hung out laundry. Today I would probably feel very deprived in that kind of living situation, but as a child I loved it. One Sunday morning my father explained in his sermon how Jesus gave His life for our sin by being crucified on a cross. He explained how He was buried in a tomb but arose from that tomb three days later, and now lives in heaven with God, His Father. He said if we wanted to be sure we would go to heaven when we died, we must ask Jesus to forgive us of our sin and invite Him into our hearts. At eight years old I figured my sin must have been fighting with my brothers or disobeying my parents. I loved my father, and I knew he wouldn't tell anything that wasn't true. I wanted to be sure I'd go to heaven when I died, so I prayed and invited Jesus to come into my heart. At that moment I became God's child.

GOD LOOKS AT OUR HEARTS

Being God's child doesn't mean we have to be perfect. God looks at our hearts. I'm reminded of the story of Samuel anointing David as the new king over Israel. God told Samuel that the person He had chosen to be the next king was from Jesse's family, so Samuel went to Bethlehem where he met with Jesse and his sons. When he saw Jesse's eldest son, Eliab, tall and handsome like King Saul had been when Samuel anointed him king, Samuel thought, "This must be the one God has chosen." But God said to Samuel: *"Do not look at his appearance or at the height of his stature, because I have refused him. For the LORD does not see as man sees; for man looks at the outward appearance, but the LORD looks at the heart."* 1 Samuel 16:7 (NKJ) Aren't we glad that God does not judge us by our outward appearance? Fortunately God only looks at our hearts. He knows what we are like. He knows that we may fail Him at times, but He also knows if the desire of our hearts is to please Him. That's what counts in His eyes. If we can just keep in mind that God's Spirit is always within us, we won't doubt that He loves us even though we are not perfect. *"....you know him, for he lives with you and will be in you."* John 14:17 (NKJ)

GROWING DEEPER

Forgiveness is an important part of growing deeper. It sets us free. Free from stress. Free from anxiety. Free from guilt. Free from painful memories. In our heads we know that Jesus came to set us free, but are we really free? *"Then you will know the truth, and the truth will set you free."* John 8:32 (NIV) We may read this scripture over and over, but it's merely head knowledge until it becomes deeply engrained in our hearts. If we ask God to search our hearts and reveal to us anything that might be hindering us from the freedom we so desire, He will do it. I know this from personal experience.

At one time or another all of us will probably face some things that are difficult. Being able to forgive is one of those things. It can be very painful. I heard a definition of forgiveness that really stuck with me. "Forgiveness is releasing love that sees no wrong." It's hard to love a person who has hurt us deeply, and even harder to 'see no wrong' in them. When God forgives us for things we have done He totally forgets about them. He doesn't see the wrong in us. Sometimes it may be necessary for us to ask forgiveness from people we have hurt, or forgive those who have hurt us. Neither one is easy! We also may need to forgive ourselves in order to be free from guilt we are carrying. Forgiveness is crucial to our spiritual and emotional health. It is a major boost in developing a close relationship with God. It's a key to freedom from the pain of our past. Unforgiveness harbored within us is like a cancer eating away inside. Chemotherapy won't get rid of it. Radiation won't get rid of it. The only way to get rid of it is to forgive.

Corrie ten Boom used to tell a story of the time she spoke at a Church in Munich in 1947. Afterwards she saw a man coming toward her that she recognized as one of the guards from Ravensbruck concentration camp. He had treated her and her sister so cruelly that her sister died. The man walked over to her and introduced himself as a former Ravensbruck guard. He told her he had since become a Christian. He looked into Corrie's eyes and said, "I know God has forgiven me for my cruelty, but, Fraulein, will you forgive me?" She instantly recalled the scripture: *"For if you forgive men when they sin against you, your heavenly Father will also forgive you. But if you do not forgive men their sins, your Father will not forgive your sins."* Matthew 6:14-15 (NIV) Reaching out to shake his extended hand, she silently prayed for God to help her forgive this man. As she did this a healing warmth flooded her body bringing tears to her eyes. Looking back at him she said, "I forgive you, brother, with all my heart."

In the natural we probably could not forgive people who have deeply hurt us, but as we allow God's Spirit to control us He will enable us to forgive. I don't know which is harder to do, asking someone to forgive you for hurting them, or forgiving someone who has hurt you. Neither is easy but both are necessary. In Colossians 3:13 it says, *"forgive whatever grievances you may have against one another. Forgive as the Lord forgave you."* God forgave us of so much. Now we must also forgive.

FORGIVING OURSELVES

In his book *Total Forgiveness* R. T. Kendall says, 'Forgiving yourself may bring about the breakthrough you have been looking for. It could set you free in ways you have never before experienced." Many Christians are able to forgive others but find it very difficult to forgive themselves. Both are equally important. If God can forgive us for what we have done, why can't we forgive ourselves? God even forgets about it but we remember it constantly and the memory condemns us. I love the scripture in Isaiah 44:22 which says, *"I have swept away your offenses like a cloud, your sins like the morning mist. Return to me, for I have redeemed you."* Think about how the clouds float away and the morning dew dries up. That's how God sees our sin. It's gone for good and He wants us to return to Him because He loves us.

As I previously mentioned, when I married Jud, my third husband, I knew I had finally found the man who would make me happy. He was a widower, a retired Air Force Colonel, very stable, a good Christian, and a great husband. What more could I ask for? However, I was so full of guilt over things I had done in my past that I lived in constant fear God would punish me by taking away my wonderful husband. This fear tormented me. I would lie awake at night thinking about it, crying silently while Jud slept.

Then one day as I was watching the 700 Club on television, Pat Robertson explained that even though we ask God's forgiveness for things we have done in our past, we still have to forgive ourselves. I had never done this so I knelt down in front of the television and prayed a prayer asking God to help me forgive myself. Immediately an indescribable peace flooded my being as all the guilt left me. I felt free at last. I knew I was forgiven. Although I have felt sad many times about things I did years ago, I have never experienced any more guilt since that moment. *"I, even I, am he who blots out your transgressions, for my own sake, and remembers your sins no more."* Isaiah 43:25 (NJK) I have learned that God does not want to punish us. He loves us too much. We don't need to keep asking for His forgiveness over and over. God forgives us the first time we ask, and then He totally forgets everything we've ever done.

TIME WITH GOD

Our journey continues! There's much more. One of the things that will make it a meaningful journey is spending time with God. You may be thinking, "How can I do that? I already go to church Sundays and Wednesdays." This is more than just going to church once or twice a week. We need to find our own places and times to spend with God. He wants to hear from us because He cares about everything that goes on in our lives. We can talk to Him while we're driving to work or when we're in the shower or getting dressed. Nothing formal, just communicating with God. If we are fortunate enough to be able to set aside time for prayer and a little Bible reading each morning, that's wonderful. But sometimes working it into our schedules before we start our busy days is a little difficult. If we have children we might not find any time until they are in bed at night. The more time we spend with God, the more we will desire it. It takes our minds off things that stress us when we focus on God and His love for us. It makes us feel energized and uplifted all day. Sort of like eating a nutritious breakfast. Our brains are sharper and we're better equipped to face the day.

Four years ago my husband and I started attending 6 AM prayer meetings at our church which was twenty minutes away. At first it took discipline to get out of bed so early and drive all the way to church, but soon it became an important part of our day. It seems that our spirits are more in control of our lives when we begin our days in prayer.

DESIRING WISDOM

When we spend time with God we usually have a list of things we ask Him for, don't we? One of the most important things we can ask for is wisdom. *"Wisdom is the principal thing; Therefore get wisdom. And in all your getting, get understanding."* Proverbs 4:7 (NKJ) We cannot obtain spiritual wisdom by merely reading a short devotional each morning, although many of them are very good. We need to read the Bible. It is full of wisdom. Finding the time to read the Bible might require a change in some of our priorities. The more we read it, the more interested we will become so we'll want to make time for it. For you women who cannot find time to sit and read, you might consider investing in tapes or CD's of the Bible so you can listen to them while you're getting dressed, driving your car, or cooking dinner. The more we put the Word into our minds, the more wisdom we will obtain. The Apostle Paul said, *"Let the word of Christ dwell in you richly."* Colossians 3:16 (NKJ)

Oral Roberts once said, "When the Word is really inside you, when it's alive and producing like it should, you can hear it." I guess it's like hearing a song and afterwards you can't get it out of your mind. It just keeps going and going. Wouldn't it be great if God's Word would affect us like that? My step-father could quote the entire Bible and in his last year before he died at 102, all he did was listen to recordings of the Bible. I'm sure the Apostle Paul would have agreed that he was letting the Word of Christ dwell richly in him. Bill Gothard said, "Wisdom is seeing life from God's point of view." It is the ability to apply biblical truths to all life situations. If we can learn to do this we probably won't be shallow any longer.

This spiritual journey we are taking with God will change our lives. We will gradually understand God's love for us and it will cause our love for Him to grow deeper and deeper. I don't think any of us want to think of ourselves as shallow. Growing deeper spiritually is a never-ending journey, but it leads to a contented, fulfilled life.

HELP ME GROW!

Lord, fill me with your love today.
Fill me so completely that there is no room within me for
doubts,
anxieties or
negative thoughts.
Let me be sensitive to Your voice,
obedient to Your leading,
content in the security of Your love.
Help me, Lord, to keep my mind
clear of clutter....
to fill it with thoughts that are uplifting.
Like vitamins for our bodies
let me only give my mind healthy, nourishing food
So I will grow
and grow
and grow.

(A page from my personal journal)

CHAPTER 4

▼

OH, MY SOUL!

Have you ever heard anyone say, "Oh, my soul?" Perhaps your grandmother—or someone about her age? You've probably heard people say that each of us has a spirit, soul and body and you wondered what a soul really is. Webster's Dictionary has many different definitions for the word "soul" and there are also many places where this word is used in the Bible with different meanings according to the Greek and Hebrew definitions. The simplest explanation I have found is this. The soul is different from the spirit and the body. It's our inner self.... our mind, will and emotions ... our intellect. It's the part of us that reasons and thinks. From infancy our minds are continually filled with all kinds of things ... some good and some bad. What we put into our minds affects our wills and emotions. The Bible tells us, *"Do not conform any longer to the pattern of this world, but be transformed by the renewing of your mind. Then you will be able to test and approve what God's will is—his good, pleasing and perfect will"*. Romans 12:2 (NIV) Even though we may have God's Spirit within us it doesn't mean our mind, will and emotions are controlled by God. It takes time to learn how to let God change our thinking. The more we read the Bible and listen to God's Word being preached, the more His Spirit within us will cause our minds to become in tune with God.

I was never known for having the most brilliant mind in the world.... actually not even in my high school. I got pretty good grades, except for biology and geometry, but I didn't make straight A's. I didn't really care because I was more interested in having fun than being smart. However, as I've grown older I've become more interested in improving my mind. Did you ever make anything out of Play-Doh? You can make one thing after the other by just remolding it into something else. That's what God wants to do with our minds after we give our lives to Him. There are things to learn and things to un-learn. If you were raised in a family that never attended church, there may be some things you find difficult to understand when you first become a Christian. It's great to ask questions. If you know someone who has a close relationship with God and is knowledgeable about the Bible, perhaps she would be willing to spend some time with you to answer any questions you may have.

I remember when a young woman named Kenna came to me in church asking for prayer to accept Jesus. After that she called me nearly every day with questions. When she started reading the Bible it raised more questions. She was hungry to learn everything she could about this new relationship she was developing and I was eager to help her in any way I could.

The word renew means "to make like new." We can't go back to when we were born and had no thoughts of our own, so how can we renew our minds? Many things influence us: our families, friends, the media, schools, jobs, movies, books, etc. Much of this influence has a negative impact on our minds. God wants to change our thoughts to conform to His way of thinking. It's not because He doesn't want us to have a will of our own, but because He knows what's best for us. *"For my thoughts are not your thoughts, neither are your ways my ways,"* *declares the LORD. As the heavens are higher than the earth, so are my ways higher* *than your ways and my thoughts than your thoughts."* Isaiah 55:8-9 (NIV)

LEARNING GOD'S THOUGHTS

Although I became God's child when I was eight years old, it doesn't mean that my thoughts were always His thoughts. Far from it! Very seldom were my thoughts His thoughts. I went through the first fifty years of my life thinking my own thoughts, making my own plans. God knew how desperately I needed to renew my mind by studying His Word, so He had a plan for me. I became friends with a woman named Chip Ricks, the Director of Christian Education at our church. She was a godly woman and a fabulous Bible teacher. She asked me if I would consider teaching a two-year women's Bible class. The first year's study was entitled, "Through the Bible in One Year," which meant teaching an overview of sixty-six books of the Bible in fifty-two weeks. What a scary thought!

Chip had been observing my spiritual growth as I attended a number of her Bible classes. She was aware that I had been a Christian since childhood, growing up in a minister's home, so she probably thought I knew a lot about the Bible.

Wrong! I was familiar with a few Bible stories I had heard all my life but I actually had not been much of a Bible student. I told Chip I did not feel qualified to teach the class, but she asked me to pray about it before I gave her my final answer. I agreed. When I prayed, I sensed God telling me, "If you are willing to teach the class I will enable you to do it." So I accepted the challenge.

Immediately I began a crash course of the entire Bible. I set up a six-foot table in my loft, bought some commentaries and other study aids, then began studying four or five days a week from morning till dinnertime. This meant declining luncheon invitations from my friends, shopping trips, and many of the fun things I enjoyed. All I had time for was studying. I didn't realize till years later how much this was renewing my mind. I was replacing old thoughts with new. I must admit, there were days I cried and felt like quitting because some parts of the Bible were so difficult to understand. But God was true to his promise. He enabled me to do it.

The first few times I stood before the Bible class to teach, I was terrified. My knees shook, my hands shook. I was sure everyone there knew more about the Bible than I did, and if I made a mistake they would all know it. How embarrassing that would be. But as the weeks went by God gave me more and more confidence until I loved teaching. When one of the ladies would tell me how much she enjoyed learning about the Bible, it thrilled my heart. I was learning to love it and wanted everyone else to love it also. Those two years of intense Bible study have made a lasting impact on my life. I will always be grateful for that opportunity to gain a deeper understanding of the Bible and learn more about God's way of thinking. I'm thankful God brought Chip Ricks into my life to be my teacher, mentor and friend. She not only taught me to love God's Word, but she challenged me to become a Bible teacher. To this day nothing gives me more pleasure than preparing to teach a Bible lesson.

NEGATIVE THINKING

Is anyone besides me guilty of thinking thoughts that are not good? Thoughts of jealousy? Thoughts of pride? Thoughts of low self-worth? Thoughts of greed? You know what I mean! We all have thoughts sometimes that we wish were not there. Our thoughts determine who we are ... they shape our character. The Apostle Paul knew how important our thought lives were when he wrote, *"Finally, brethren, whatever things are true, whatever things are noble, whatever things are just, whatever things are pure, whatever things are lovely, whatever things are of good report, if there is any virtue and if there is anything praiseworthy—medi-*

tate on these things" Philippians 4:8 (NKJ) I wish I could say all my thoughts were like this verse of scripture. I'm working on it though.... with God's help.

Jerry Bridges in *Pursuit of Holiness* wrote, "Holiness begins in our minds and works out to our actions. This being true, what we allow to enter our minds is critically important." What do we allow to enter our minds? Would God approve of all the movies, television shows, books, magazines, and music that enter our minds? At a time when I was discouraged with the condition of my spiritual life, I prayed that God would show me what was wrong. I immediately sensed Him telling me I was watching some things on TV that were filling my mind with the wrong kinds of thoughts. I had to admit it was true, so I began to be more selective about what I watched. Before long I noticed a difference in my relationship with God. I felt a closeness I had not experienced before.

Have you ever felt like Satan was attacking you by putting fear, doubts and untruths into your mind? He does that! Sometimes we have relationships that are ruined simply because we have unfounded thoughts in our minds about people. Doubts and fears have kept many people from achieving their hearts' desires in life. Feelings of rejection or poor self-image can make us feel so inadequate we aren't willing to do things God has planned for us. *"As a man thinks in his heart, so does he become."* Proverbs 23:7 (NIV) If we think we can't, we can't! Let's not allow Satan to cheat us out of the good things God has for us. The way to get rid of these damaging thoughts is to read the Word and ask God to start replacing the negative thoughts with positive ones. We can't prevent bad thoughts from entering our minds, but we can prevent them from staying there. God's Word is a sword, a weapon, which we can use to fight our enemy. The more we read it, the more able we are to defeat Satan when he tries to fill our minds with negative thoughts. It's up to us to keep these thoughts out of our minds.

I must admit it's much easier to tell someone else to do this than to do it myself. Once when we were selling our house the deal fell through. We had already moved and were paying two house payments, so this was not good news. When we went to bed that night my husband, Jud, was asleep within seconds, but I lay there thinking "what if" thoughts till about midnight. It's easy to say, "Don't be anxious," but doing it ourselves is a little harder. We know God's in control, but it's difficult to be confident that God has the situation under control when things aren't going the way we want them to. We can practice not being anxious by filling our minds with positive thoughts and remembering what God tells us in His Word.

PRESERVING OUR MINDS

All of us want to keep a sharp mind as we grow older. Prior to writing this book I took a survey of about 100 women asking them, "What are your concerns about growing older?" The leading answer was, "Losing mental abilities." When we start forgetting things it's sort of scary. Some of us notice this happening as early as our forties.... some much later. We wonder if we are going to have a problem as we get older. If we tell our friends about it we'll most likely find that they are experiencing the same thing, so it's usually nothing to worry about. Many people have "senior moments" long before they're old. If this happens to you, a good Bible verse to remember is Proverbs 10:7. *"The memory of the righteous will be a blessing."* (NIV) I recently heard a cute joke about memory loss. Only those of you who have experienced what I call "Senior moments" can appreciate this.

"An employee returned to the same downstairs office three times in a matter of minutes. After the fourth trip to retrieve something else she had forgotten, the absent-minded woman muttered, 'Pretty soon I'll be able to hide my own Easter eggs.'" We can joke about memory loss but we still might entertain thoughts like, "Am I going to end up with Alzheimer's?" Not likely! From all I've read on the subject, only a very small percentage of people are actually afflicted with Alzheimer's disease but most of us will experience occasional memory loss. Once I read an article stating that anything containing aluminum could cause you to have Alzheimer's. I wasn't scared but just to be on the safe side, I replaced all our deodorant and baking powder containing aluminum. It is good to do everything we can to preserve our minds.

There are things we can do to keep our minds sharp as we grow older. One is keep them active ... don't let them stagnate. Reading is a good thing. Romance novels may be entertaining, and we ladies love to be entertained, however, it might be wiser to read things that inspire us to improve our lives. We might even desire to take some classes at a local college. When I took two art classes in a nearby college, I was the oldest person in the room, but learning about design and drawing was a challenge for me. Being a choleric personality type, I love challenges. I was thrilled when I received A's in both classes. One thing nice about being older, you get to do things you want to do rather than things you have to do.

Trying to do things differently than we're used to is good for our minds. Try brushing your teeth with your left hand if you're right-handed, or when you go to church or the grocery store, try driving a different route. Anything to keep that mind working.

Whenever I have spare time instead of allowing my mind to be idle, I enjoy working crossword puzzles or Cryptograms in the newspaper. Lately I've also tried Suduko, but it's a real challenge. Now don't laugh, but I keep a basket full of puzzles beside the toilet so I can pick one up every time I'm using the bathroom. You can tell I'm a Type A personality who doesn't want to waste time. I also like to play word games such as Scrabble, UpWords and Anagrams if I can find someone to play with. (My husband doesn't care for word games.) If you're super intelligent you might also try games like Trivia Pursuit or Bible Trivia. I find them a little too challenging!

CHALLENGING OUR BRAINS

We all need to do things that challenge our brains. It's easy to say, "Oh, I can't do that, it's too difficult." But you may be surprised what you can do. Don't let those brains cells die, keep them working. About twelve years ago, I decided to take on the computer challenge. I knew it was going to be a big challenge for me but I really wanted to do it. I didn't have any extra money to buy a computer, so I decided to pray about it. The main reason I wanted a computer was to type my Bible study lessons, which I had been typing on an old IBM typewriter. When I prayed, God put a idea into my mind that I'm sure was God's because I would have never have come up with this idea on my own. He said, "Since you don't play your piano any longer, you could sell it to buy the computer." I loved having a piano in my home. Even if I didn't play it any longer, it was a beautiful piece of furniture. The living room just wouldn't be complete without it. There had hardly ever been a time in my life when I did not have a piano, so I couldn't imagine being without it. I grew up in a musical family and took piano lessons for much of my childhood, although I never became an accomplished pianist. The more I thought about selling it the more I realized God was right. I didn't play it so why not sell it to buy the computer I wanted? So that's what I did!

Learning to operate a computer took a lot of patience and discipline. I hired a tutor, read books and tutorials that came with the computer, and practiced, practiced, practiced. Finally I was able to learn enough about it to enjoy it. Now I love it! Can't imagine being without it.

Next I tackled the Internet and e-mails. A new challenge! Connecting to the internet has opened all kinds of new learning opportunities. I've found recipes, word definitions, addresses, historical facts, Bible helps, weather forecasts, maps, graphics, just to name a few. I can even pay bills on-line. One time I wanted some information about Michaelangelo for a talk I was preparing and I not only found information about his life, but there were also pictures of his paintings in the Sistene Chapel that were marvelous.

Longfellow once said, "That tree is very old but I never saw prettier blossoms on it than it now bears. That tree grows new wood each year. Like that apple tree I try to grow a little new wood each year." We can always learn new things. It's a good way to keep our minds active.

FREE WILL

When God created us He gave us a free will. He didn't want us to be puppets on a string, unable to make decisions on our own. Having a will of our own can be a good thing, but it can also make it difficult to comply with God's will for our lives. Society teaches us to think about ourselves first and always do what's best for us. This influences which schools we attend, the careers we choose, the men we marry, the kind of houses we live in or cars we drive. It's all about us! When we make a choice to let God be in control of our lives, it's difficult to quit doing our own thing and let Him influence our decisions. Even though we ask God for His direction, we often struggle getting our own wills out of the way. Consequently many of the plans we make are not God's plans. *"Many are the plans in a man's heart, but it is the LORD'S purpose that prevails."* Proverbs 19:21 (NIV) I wish I could say I have always chosen God's will rather than my own, but even though I accepted Jesus as my Savior at a young age, most of my life I was the one in control, not God. I'm glad we serve a loving, forgiving God who is always willing to give us another chance.

About twenty years ago I went to a CLASS (Christian Leaders, Authors and Speakers Services) seminar taught by Florence Littauer, where I learned about the different personality types. For the first time in my life I became aware that I had a strong, controlling Choleric personality. It's no wonder I had such a difficult time relinquishing control to God.

I recall a time as a teenager when my mother asked me to sing a duet with her in church. In retrospect, I'm sure she had a reason for selecting the song we sang, *Sweet Will of God.* The words of the first line were, "My stubborn will at last I've yielded." Mother was well aware of how stubborn I was and how much I needed to experience the sweet will of God.

Mother once told me that when I was a small child she observed me trying to untie my shoestrings and offered to help. My response was, "No, I do it myself." I was independent, headstrong and unteachable as a child, as well as most of my life. Finally at age fifty I became aware of my need to let God take control of my life. I asked His forgiveness and invited Him to take over my controlling spirit so

I could become the woman I was destined to be. Rightfully by this time in my life I should have been a godly woman full of wisdom, but instead I was just getting started in my spiritual growth. I had so much to learn!

As soon as I surrendered my will to God wonderful things began to happen. God made many changes in me and from that day till now it's been constant growth. Everything didn't change overnight, however. It was a process, but it's been wonderful! This has become the happiest, most fulfilling season of my life.

EMOTIONS

Emotions are also part of our souls and they play a very important role in our lives. Without emotions we would be like robots. How boring would that be? Anger, sadness, fear, and guilt are inevitable emotions we all experience at some time in our lives, but they are not ones that we want to control us. In his book, *Deadly Emotions,* Dr. Don Colbert says that many diseases are caused from allowing the wrong kind of emotions to control us.

Anger can be an emotion that is destructive if we don't learn to control it. I once knew a man who had so much anger in him that he was abusive to his wife and children. They eventually chose to leave him and he was a very sad man. Anger is acceptable in some instances but we have to choose not to let it control us causing us to do things which hurt other people.

HAPPINESS is an emotion—a feeling. It's the kind of feeling we all desire. To be happy means to be satisfied or content. How many of us ever achieve this? It seems we always want something more than we have. We want whatever makes us feel good, thinking it will make us happy. Brunettes want to be blonde, short people want to be tall. Pale, freckle-face people (like me) want to have olive skin. If we live in a $100,000 house, we want a $200,000 one. If we drive a Honda we'd rather have a Lexus. Most of us want something other than what we have. That's human nature. We are emotional people and often we allow our feelings to control us. We think if we have a lot of material things we will be satisfied and content. Sometimes it takes years before we realize it's only God who can bring us the satisfaction and contentment we desire. *"Delight yourself in the LORD and he will give you the desires of your heart."* Psalms 37:4. But there's a catch to this. If our desires are only for material things like big cars and houses, beautiful expensive clothes, or recognition for things we've done, we may not get these things. Why? Because we may not be delighting in the Lord. We're probably delighting in ourselves. There's nothing wrong with having material things if they aren't more important than pleasing God.

When we ladies fall in love with "Mr. Right," we want to spend time with him getting to know him. We want to do everything possible to please him. Nothing's too good for that wonderful man! That's how we should be with God—love to spend time with Him, get to know Him, delight in Him. Gradually we'll discover that the things we desire for ourselves will be the things He wants to give us. Just as parents only want the best for their children, God wants the very best for us.

JOY is also an emotion which is very good for us. The Bible teaches about it … doctors recommend it. The Bible says, *"A merry heart does good, like medicine."* Proverbs 17:22 (NKJ) Joy is different from happiness. Happiness is temporary— brought about by something we're experiencing or what's around us. Joy is lasting—a feeling of contentment deep inside—an inner sense of value, purpose, fulfillment and satisfaction. Joy does not come from circumstances—it's a choice. If adversity happens in our lives, we can choose not to let it steal our joy. Billy Sunday said, "If you have no joy in your religion, there's a leak in your Christianity somewhere."

FEELINGS

Have you ever noticed how feelings can sometimes deceive us? If we live by feelings, we will be high one minute and the very next minute we can sink into a pit of despair. We also are likely to spend a lot of time feeling guilty about things we have done in our past. This can cause feelings of depression. Once we have accepted Jesus into our lives it's important to remind ourselves that when He died on the cross He took our guilt upon Himself. Once we accept that fact we can have peaceful feelings.

When you ride a roller coaster you may experience a feeling of excitement or you may be afraid. Two very different feelings! Getting kissed for the first time by the man you love will cause you to experience a wonderful feeling—passion. Passion is great as long as it doesn't control us and cause us to make wrong choices. Some people tend to let feelings play too important a role in their relationship with God. It isn't necessary to have "spiritual goose bumps" in order to know that God is present. He's with us all the time. God created us with all these different feelings, but sometimes we don't know how to control them and need God's help. It's our choice what we do with our feelings.

All of us want to live a long, happy life and in order to do this we need to prepare by taking good care of our spirits, souls and bodies … all three. We've all seen people who focus on their bodies, but maybe they neglect their spirits and souls. There's also people who focus so much on their spirits that they neglect their bodies. We need balance. We've already talked about our spiritual lives in chapter three and souls in this chapter. Next let's consider how to take care of our bodies so they will stay in good shape as long as we live.

CHAPTER 5

▼

LOVE THAT BOD!

Have you ever wondered what Eve's body looked like? I'm sure it must have been more than a "10." Adam was probably quite a hunk also. Eve didn't have to be concerned with gaining weight from what she ate, but I guess she was like many of us in that she was tempted to eat something she shouldn't. When we eat "forbidden fruit" it usually only affects us, but when Eve took one bite of that apple God told her not to eat, she affected all of us. She set into motion the aging process we all have to deal with today. Don't you wonder what it might have been like if she had been obedient? Would all of us have perfect bodies with no wrinkles, cellulite, unwanted fat cells, arthritis, acid reflux, or any kind of disease? That would be great! But she sinned, and now all of us have less than perfect bodies. It takes a lot of care to keep them looking good and functioning properly. Our bodies were given to us for a short time in comparison to eternity, but we are responsible for keeping them in good shape so we can fulfill our destiny while we're here on earth. *"… do you not know that your body is the temple of the Holy Spirit who is in you, whom you have from God, and you are not your own? For you were bought at a price; therefore glorify God in your body and in your spirit, which are God's."* 1 Corinthians 6:19 (NKJ)

LISTEN TO OUR BODIES

As we get older we don't like to admit we have less stamina than when we were young, because in our mind's eye we visualize ourselves as still being like a twenty-year-old. But eventually we have to accept the fact we're not twenty any longer. We must learn to listen to what our bodies are saying to us. If we feel tired, maybe it's because we are too busy. We're not allowing ourselves enough time to relax and do fun things. We just work, work, work. About ten years ago my husband and I bought a time-share in Branson, MO. It's one of the best investments we ever made. When we were at home we stayed busy all the time, especially during the seven years Jud's mother lived with us, so Branson was our getaway—a place to relax and have fun. Jud is a very organized person with a list for everything he's planning to do for the next two or three days, but when we went to Branson he was totally different. His list didn't control us, we would go to bed and get up later, we would watch movies or take naps in the afternoon, we'd eat in restaurants or in the condo, whichever we felt like doing. It was wonderful. Then when we got home we both felt refreshed and ready to get back to our busy schedules.

It's healthy for everyone to take a break from busyness. If we are tired frequently, there could be a reason for it. More often than not it is nothing serious, simply that our schedules are too busy or we may need to take vitamins. The older we get the more we need to pay attention to how we feel. When we are tired we get grumpy and don't enjoy things we normally love to do. Sometimes we don't even enjoy our husbands or our children, and that's not good.

When I was out of town for four days attending a writers' conference I returned home to find that I had a luncheon and a potluck dinner to attend on the same week end. I also had promised to watch my friend's daughter compete in horseback riding. There was something scheduled every day and evening for two weeks. Just thinking about it made me feel exhausted. There was nothing wrong with me physically, I just needed some time to slow down and relax … to rest my body and mind. On Sunday after church service, we ate a nice brunch in a restaurant, then I spent the rest of the day reading and resting. That was all I needed to be refreshed and ready to go again. If you're tired continually, there could be a physical reason for it. If a day of rest doesn't revive you, it might be wise to see your doctor for a checkup. There are a number of physical conditions that can cause fatigue, but growing older is not a reason to be tired if your body is in good condition.

REDUCE STRESS

After Jud retired from the Air Force in 1978, he worked five years for an aerospace company. The work was very stressful, sometimes requiring him to be there six or seven days a week. I was concerned about the effect the stress was having on his body. One day while he was at work I attended an art class in a nearby town. One of the women in my class told us she came home one day and found her husband lying in the middle of the street. He had suffered a severe stroke which left him like a vegetable. She said he had been working on a very stressful job, much like Jud's, and she believed this could have been the cause of the stroke. I immediately thought of the stress Jud was experiencing on his job. I could hardly wait until he came home from work to tell him this story. I suggested he consider quitting his job and we could scale down our lifestyle to enable us to live on his Air Force retirement. Although he isn't a person to show much emotion, I could tell he was relieved. The very next day he resigned. We sold our big house and bought a two-bedroom condo. Although he hadn't complained about the stress, I'm sure he realized it was taking its toll on his body. Since then we have enjoyed a wonderful life together. I believe the stress-less years since he resigned have not only given him a more relaxed life, but a prolonged, healthier life. It's important that we listen to our bodies if we want to enjoy our older years.

JUST SAY NO

No, is not a bad word! I have found that as I've grown older, it has become much easier to say no when people ask me to do things I don't have time for or don't want to do. We are always being asked to do things that take up our time and energy. Many times we consent because we feel that's what good Christian women should do. That's not necessarily so. The more we mature spiritually the more we learn to listen to the Lord's direction about activities in which we become involved. In most churches there are constant needs for women to serve, e.g. teachers for ladies' Bible studies, Sunday School teachers, nursery workers, making goodies for bake sales, hospital visitation, working in the church book store—and the list goes on. If you have children in school or sports you undoubtedly have been asked to help with bake sales or manning the concession stands. Our time can be all used up doing good things, but then we get stressed because we don't have enough time to handle things at home like helping the children with homework, laundry, cooking, cleaning, etc. It's very easy to get too much on our plates if we don't learn to say no! Just because you volunteered to be a teacher for the six-year-olds in Sunday School, it does not mean you are committed to it until you die. Our desires change as we get older. As a young mother we may love working with small children, but when we're fifty or sixty we might prefer teaching an adult class or working in the church book store. God always has something important for us to do that suits us.

A few years ago Jud and I volunteered to help care for small children at a meeting of the Division of Family Services while the foster parents attended the class. It wasn't something we especially wanted to do, but they really needed helpers. We were the only adults caring for about twenty infants and toddlers. One child screamed constantly if she wasn't being held so, since there were no adult-sized chairs, I walked around holding her the entire time. I went home each evening with a terrible backache. After doing this three times, I finally had the courage to say "Sorry, this is not for me."

EAT, DRINK AND BE HEALTHY

The foods we eat can make a great difference in how we look and feel. Every magazine, newspaper or book we read about health tells us something different when it comes to healthy diets. It can be very confusing. We all know that fad diets are not good for a lifestyle, although they may work for quick weight loss. There's much more to consider than merely keeping our weight down. Learning about nutrition is very important so we can avoid foods and beverages that are harmful to our bodies.

HEALTHY EATING CHANGED MY LIFE

In 2001 I was diagnosed with Polymyalgia, a disease which causes pain in the muscles and joints all over the body. The doctor prescribed one of the leading pain medications, but it had undesirable side effects, in addition to costing $120 per month. I prayed earnestly for God to heal me, I listened to tapes and read books about healing, but the more I prayed the more I sensed God directing me to contact a friend who had been healed of a serious illness simply by changing her diet. Of course, I would rather have had a miraculous healing. That would have been easy. But I knew God was leading me to a different pathway of healing. I began a vegetarian diet (no meat, dairy, white flour, caffeine or sugar), eating mostly raw fruits and vegetables. In addition I took daily doses of powdered barley grass and carrots. Gradually I noticed physical problems I had endured for a number of years were gone, such as hypoglycemia and chronic sinusitis. It took a little longer for the polymyalgia to leave, but it wasn't long until I was pain free. What a blessing! When people ask, "How can you eat that kind of weird diet?" I just tell them I remember the pain I used to have, and that makes being a vegetarian easy. I must admit I now eat fish and eggs, so I am not a true vegetarian—I'm what's known as a flexatarian.

I'm aware that God heals some people instantly, but I'm grateful He chose to heal me by leading me into a healthy way of eating. Not only will I be healthy in my older years, but I will be able to share what I have learned with other people who are interested in having better health. Although I'm past sixty, I get up at 5 AM each day, work out at a gym four or five days a week, and have plenty of energy. I'm healthier, and feel better, than I when I was a younger woman.

SUGAR ADDICTION

Signs of the Times Magazine published my article *My Sweet Struggle* telling about my personal battle with sugar. I grew up as a chubby child loving sweets. I well remember my eighth birthday when I told my mother all I wanted for my birthday was a banana split. In those days banana splits cost twenty-five cents but my father's meager income as a minister did not allow for such luxuries very often. However, my birthday was cause to celebrate and Mother and I went to the neighborhood ice cream parlor together. I ordered a huge banana split. When the waitress set it down in front of me, I was in heaven. There were three big scoops of ice cream: chocolate, vanilla and strawberry, topped with pineapple and chocolate sauces and an enormous dollop of whipped cream. I savored every delicious spoonful of my banana split, thankful I didn't have to share any of it with my four brothers.

All my life I had loved sweets and ate them at every opportunity. Then at age forty-seven I had a rude awakening. I was diagnosed with severe hypoglycemia, the next step to diabetes I was told. The effects of sugar in my body had caused me to feel so terrible that I was more than willing to go on the sugar-free diet my doctor recommended. However, once I started feeling better I would gradually start eating sweets again, thinking I could control my low blood sugar by just eating sugar occasionally until I started feeling badly, then abstain until I felt well again. I was a human yo-yo, up one week and down the next. To satisfy my desire for sweets I bought every artificially-sweetened cookie, cake, muffin or candy available. Although I was not eating much sugar, I was consuming a lot of calories so my weight began to soar.

One night I had a dream that I knew was from God. He told me that my body was the temple of the Holy Spirit and I was abusing it. He went on to say, "If you want Me to use you in ministry, you must take care of your body." I knew exactly what He meant. No more sugar! I was able to abstain for a few weeks, but that was all. I was addicted! I couldn't live without it (so I thought).

One day while grocery shopping I bought a box of frozen honey buns reasoning with myself that I'd put them in the freezer and once in a while for a special treat I'd thaw one to eat. All the way to the car I thought about those honey buns. By the time I put the groceries into the trunk I was like an alcoholic searching for a bottle of booze. I wanted those honey buns. I dug down into the bag, found the honey buns, and put them on the car seat beside me. By the time I arrived home, I had eaten all four partially frozen honey buns.

It took over a year before I began to take seriously what God had told me in my dream. On March 8, 1990 (I know the exact date because I wrote it in my journal and put stars all over the page so I would never forget it) I made a commitment to God to give up everything made with refined sugar, especially my favorites: Milky Ways, miniature pecan pies, and honey buns. I have kept my commitment most of the time and it has not only made me healthier, but it has improved my relationship with God. I've heard people say "When you quit eating sugar you lose the desire for it." Maybe that's true for some people, but not for me. When someone offers me a piece of gooey chocolate cake, although I'd love to eat it, I think about my commitment to God and say, "No thank you." Sugar is addictive, so we need God's help to kick the habit..

HEALTHY BEVERAGES

On my journey to good health I have learned many interesting things. One is the importance of what we drink, or maybe I should say what we don't drink. Most of us are used to drinking coffee, tea, soft drinks, and milk, but very little water. I was amazed when I learned what a negative effect these beverages have on our bodies.

Coffee and Tea: I really enjoy a good cup of coffee or a glass of iced tea. When I quit drinking everything containing caffeine I could tell I was addicted because I had a headache for four days. I now enjoy a cup of decaf coffee nearly every morning, but I'm no longer addicted to caffeine. A six-ounce cup of coffee contains about 120 mg of caffeine, the same amount of tea contains 100 mg, but decaf coffee only has 18 mg. I was surprised to read that most adults consume 300 mg or more of caffeine before lunch, often on an empty stomach. Research shows this can produce anxiety, irritability and even panic. The way to tell if you are drinking too much coffee or tea, according to Dr. Mary Ruth Swope, is to give it up for two or three days and see if you experience fatigue, anxiety, insomnia, racing of the heart, finger tremors, imperfect balance or a sense of dread. If you do, you are addicted to caffeine. Caffeine also causes blood-sugar swings, acid imbalance and mineral depletion. There are such mixed opinions about the effects of caffeine that it's hard to know what to do … drink coffee or not drink coffee. Most reports agree that we should not consume large amounts of it.

Milk: Many magazines have pictures of white-mustached celebrities touting the benefits of milk. Since I'm lactose intolerant it didn't bother me much when I read a lot of negative things about the effect milk has on our bodies. Dr. George Malkmus says in *God's Way to Ultimate Health,* "We are told milk is the perfect food and it is needed for calcium. We are not told that the pasteurizing of milk (heating it to temperatures of 160 degrees or higher) changes the calcium to an inorganic form, which cannot be assimilated by the body." Maybe that explains why so many babies cannot tolerate milk.

Years ago when I joined Weight Watchers, I started eating dairy products as part of their recommended diet. I discovered I was lactose intolerant, so now I use either rice or soy milk. When eating in restaurants I take Lactaid pills with me in case something contains dairy products.. If you're a milk-drinker I can only suggest you research this matter for yourself.

Soft drinks: Coffee is not the only source of caffeine. Most soft drinks contain caffeine, as well as sugar, or artificial sweeteners, plus many are high in sodium. Six-ounce bottles of Coca-Cola contain 40 mg. of caffeine, Dr. Pepper: 38 mg., Pepsi: 36 mg.

Water: This is what we need the most, but what we drink least. There are so many benefits to water, especially if it's pure. Distilled is good because there's no chlorine, fluoride, sodium or bacteria in it. Water is the most important nutrient for the human body. Approximately two-thirds of our body weight is water. People can live for forty days without food, but only three to five days without water. Dr. Don Colbert in his book, *What Would Jesus Eat,* says "Water is necessary for nearly every bodily function, including circulation, digestion, absorption, and excretion. Water is vital for carrying nutrients to all cells of the body. An adequate intake is essential to remove waste products from the body via the bloodstream and excretory organs." Did you know that by drinking five glasses of water a day you cut the risk of breast cancer by 79%?

Most authorities on nutrition say we need to drink eight glasses of water a day. That's a lot! If you try to do this, you probably will find that you have to eliminate some of the other beverages you have been drinking to make room for the water. It may be difficult at first, but try it gradually. I now find that outside of an occasional cup of decaf coffee or herb tea, water is my only beverage. Just keep thinking, "This water is making me healthy."

LOOKIN' GOOD!

As a child I always liked the part of *Snow White* where the Wicked Witch looked into the mirror and asked "Mirror, mirror on the wall. Who's the fairest one of all?" and instead of seeing herself she'd see the beautiful Snow White. We all like to look into a mirror and see a beautiful image. We want to be "the fairest one of all." The older we get the harder it is to see the image we desire in our mirrors. We have to work at it. Making ourselves look attractive perks us up. When we look bad we feel bad and it has a negative effect on our whole day. It's important to do whatever we can to look our best.

Skin: Not all of us have beautiful olive complexion. I, being a redhead, have pale skin with lots of freckles. Growing up I hated it. I put lemon juice and all kinds of bleach cream on my face, but nothing worked. I was still covered with freckles. As I've grown older I've learned to accept them (but never liking them). Taking good care of my skin has become very important to me. Staying out of the sun, using lots of creams and not washing my face with soap have helped preserve it. I must admit I'm not overjoyed with the each new set of wrinkles, or the occasional whiskers that grow on my chin, but even though it takes me longer than it used to getting ready in the mornings, I take the time to use all the powder and paint I need to make me look good. Even if I'm staying at home all day wearing sweats, if my face and hair look good I enjoy the day much more.

It's a good idea to cleanse our faces every night with a good quality cleansing cream instead of soap. NEVER GO TO BED WITH YOUR MAKEUP STILL ON! If we have dry skin, (as I do) it helps to use a moisture cream under our makeup in the daytime and again before going to bed. It isn't necessary to pay high prices for our cosmetics if we are on a limited budget, but it's good to try buying things with as many natural ingredients as possible. Wearing makeup that makes us look radiant and attractive is good for our self-image.

Hair: As a child I did not like being a redhead because of all the teasing that went with it, but in my older years I have enjoyed my red hair, at least until the gray came along. That's when I started adding color to my hair, and I am determined to go to my grave as a redhead. It's important to find a hair stylist we like and stick with her so she will become familiar with the way we like our hair. It helps to keep up with modern styles instead of wearing the same hairdo for twenty years. If our hair has lost the vibrancy it once had there's nothing wrong with having color put on it. It makes us feel (and look) younger. A good quality shampoo and conditioner are important even though they may cost a few dollars more.

Body: Diet and Exercise Nobody likes to hear those two words: diet and exercise. But they can both become an important part of our everyday lives. If we don't like what we see in the mirror due to some extra pounds added through the years, we need to do something about it. When I was in my sugar-craving "honey bun" days I really put on the pounds so I enrolled at Weight Watchers where it took me a whole year to lose twenty pounds. It's amazing what twenty pounds will do for our self image. When I saw snapshots taken before and after the weight loss I decided "Thin is definitely better!" Now when I gain two or three pounds I quickly start cutting back on fattening foods until those pounds are gone. I recently heard that in parts of Africa women are so skinny that a bride-to-be is given ninety days before the wedding to fatten her up. Their men like women with lots of meat on their bones. I can't imagine trying to gain weight because all my life I've struggled to keep it off.

I don't know anyone who really likes to exercise. It may never become our favorite activity, but it's important to our bodies' health. I didn't start a regular exercise program until I was over sixty. When I noticed my legs were getting weak making it difficult to get up from a sitting position, I remembered my mother having a similar problem when she was about my age. We'd have to pull her up if she sat on the couch. I did not want that to happen to me so I enrolled in a gym class doing water aerobics at first, then gradually adding other exercises. When I started using the various machines I was self-conscious about only walking 2.8 on the treadmill when the woman next to me was going 3.9 on an incline. On all the machines I had to start at a very low number. I hoped no one noticed. Gradually my arms and legs became stronger and I could increase my numbers on all the exercise machines.

There was a survey taken of women between the ages of 50–84 to find out what they thought they should do to be prepared for a longer, more meaningful life. The thing they wanted to do least was exercise and change their eating habits. Statistics show that women over eighty-five make up the fastest growing group in the world, so it's vitally important to keep our bodies healthy if we don't want to end up in a nursing home.

Exercise is important for muscle retention, bone density, gallstones, heart, blood pressure, and stress. Some of the benefits are: agility, posture, detoxification, alertness, weight loss, eliminating constipation and better digestion. It will even help with menopause. Dr. JoAnn Pinkerton, director of the University of Virginia's Midlife Health Center says "Exercise is the best thing a woman can do for herself at midlife. It improves heart function, so we have less chance of cardiac disease. It helps us think better, it decreases our risk of breast cancer, it helps our moods, it lessens the likelihood of depression and it increases energy and protects our bones." Researchers at the University of Texas Southwestern Medical Center showed that 30 to 35 minutes on a treadmill, three to five times a week, reduced moderate depressive symptoms by almost 50%.

Going to an exercise class with a friend makes it more fun. It can be intimidating if we're overweight when we see women with gorgeous bodies in spandex gym clothes. However, we shouldn't let that stop us. When I started I was a little over-weight so I bought myself a bright, loose-fitting t-shirt and some cute gym pants that looked good on me. Then I chose a time that fit into my schedule so I would be able to go consistently. Calvin Coolidge once said "Nothing in the world can take the place of persistence." I was persistent! Now my husband and I go to our gym four or five mornings a week. I realize that may not be easy for some of you to do because of your busy schedules. Since we're retired it's easier for us than for people who have jobs, but it's amazing how many working people come early in the morning on their way to work. They do their workout, take a shower, then head to work. Even though I've been doing it for years, I still think every day, "I'd much rather stay at home with a good cup of coffee and the morning news-paper." Although I don't especially want to exercise, I always feel better physically and mentally when it's over.

Clothes: Do you wear clothes that make your body look its best? How many of you have three sets of clothes in your closet? Ones that fit, ones that are too small and ones the are too big. One thing I learned a long time ago is not to keep clothes in my closet that don't fit, are out of date, or don't look good on me. It's better to wear one outfit over and over that looks great on you rather than clothes that make you feel dowdy. If you are on a tight budget try to go shopping when there are sales, but take a friend with you who will give you her candid opinion if something isn't becoming to you. Buy colors that bring out the beauty of your eyes and brighten up your complexion. I've tried on dresses that I thought made me look matronly and the clerk told me how beautiful I looked. That's her job, but don't believe her if you have any doubts about whether or not the dress becomes you. You need someone to tell you the truth. You want your body to look good.

INNER BEAUTY

We would all probably like to have beautiful bodies, but there's another kind of beauty that's important. It's inner beauty. As I opened a box of Black Cherry Berry tea by Celestial Seasonings, I read something I liked written by Elizabeth Cady Stanton on "Inner Beauty."

> "When it is only through age that one gathers wisdom and experience, why this endless struggle to seem young? Remember that beauty works from within; it cannot be put on and off like a garment, and it depends far more on the culture of the intellect, the tastes, sentiment, and affections of the soul than the color of the hair, eyes or complexion. Be kind, noble generous, well-mannered, be true to yourselves and your friends, and the soft lines of

these tender graces and noble virtues will reveal themselves in the face. We cannot be one thing and look another. There are indelible marks in every face showing the real life within."

When I think of inner beauty the first person who comes to mind is Mother Teresa. She was not outwardly beautiful, yet no one has ever been such a beautiful person. She said "Keep the joy of loving God in your heart and share this joy with all you meet, especially your family." She showed the joy of loving God wherever she went. She also said, "Like Jesus, we belong to the world living not for ourselves but for others. The joy of the Lord is our strength." If God made us with a beautiful face, body and hair, we are blessed, but that's outer beauty. No matter what we look like on the outside, we can have inner beauty. It comes from God. Some call it "The Beauty of Holiness." It's different from natural beauty, it won't fade away with age. When God looks at us He doesn't see the same image we see in the mirror. He sees us as perfect, inside and out, probably like Eve the day He created her. My prayer for all of us is to let the beauty of holiness shine forth.

Is it wrong to love our bodies? Absolutely not! God gave us these bodies and it's His desire for us to take good care of them. So love that bod! Pamper it! Keep it healthy and strong so you can have a long, enjoyable life. Remember that your body is the temple of the Holy Spirit, so be the very best "temple" you can possibly be.

CHAPTER 6

▼

IS THAT YOU, GOD?

Have you ever heard God speak to you? God speaks to everyone, but quite often we don't hear Him because we're not listening. My husband sometimes speaks to me while I'm reading the paper, watching TV or working at my computer. I don't hear what he says because my mind is on something else. That's how we are with God, too preoccupied to hear Him.

In the Bible there are stories of God speaking to people. Some listened, but some did not. He spoke to Moses with an audible voice from a burning bush. He spoke to Cain after he murdered his brother Abel. He spoke to Noah and told him to build an ark. Think of the consequences if Noah had not been listening. He and all of his family, plus all the animals God had ever created, would have perished. God told Abraham that he and his wife, Sarai, would have a baby when Abraham was 100 and Sarai was 90. That could make you question if you really heard God correctly. All these people, and many others, heard God speaking to them.

There were many different ways God spoke to people in the Bible: by audible voice, visions, dreams and even angelic messengers. He once spoke to King Belshazzar by writing on the wall with what looked like a man's hand. He also spoke through a donkey. Now that would get our attention! Although God can speak to us in many ways, the most common way is through what we call "a still small voice." It's usually just thoughts He puts into our minds.

RECOGNIZING GOD'S VOICE

How do we learn to recognize someone's voice? By spending time with them listening to them talk. People who have been married a long time never have a problem recognizing their mate's voice because they know each other very well … they have an intimate relationship. If we want to hear God's voice we must develop an intimate relationship with him. The more time we spend alone with Him, quietly listening to His voice, the more familiar it will become to us. Many of us talk instead of listening when we have our quiet time with God. That doesn't allow us to hear His voice. It's important to become listeners. The Bible talks about how the sheep follow the Shepherd because they know his voice. *"his sheep follow him because they know his voice."* John 10:4 (NIV) God's voice isn't usually audible to our natural ears, but it's very clear to the ears of our spirits. When we read about God speaking to Moses, Abraham, Jacob, Noah and many others, we don't doubt that they heard His voice, and yet many of us find it hard to believe that God will speak to us.

If we had heard a voice coming out of a burning bush like Moses did, would we have believed it was God? During the forty years Moses tended his father-in-law's sheep he must have developed an intimate relationship with God, so he was quick to recognize God's voice. When God called his name he immediately responded, "Here I am." If we had a dream like Jacob's when he saw angels going up and down a stairway with God standing at the top, would we have said, "Oh, that was just a weird dream?" or would we have recognized it was God speaking to us?

Have you ever had a thought come into your mind about doing something nice for someone other than your family or close friends? That could have been God speaking to you. Or have you ever had someone's name keep coming into your mind for no apparent reason? Maybe God is alerting you to pray for that person. Years ago I had a strong urge to pray for my brother-in-law, Bill. I felt it was from God so I prayed fervently for about five minutes not knowing why, except that I felt God was telling me to do it. The next day Bill told me he came very close to having a tragic accident at work. I was so glad God impressed me to pray for him. We need to practice listening so we can learn to recognize God's voice. Then we won't have to wonder, "Is that You, God?"

We all lead such busy lives it's hard to be quiet enough to hear God's voice, but the more time we spend alone with Him, the more we will hear Him speak. We may need to shut off the TV or the stereo and just be quiet. When I am alone in my car I hardly ever turn on the radio or CD's anymore because I want to be listening if God should speak to me. Be ready—be listening—God will speak to you.

When I came to the place that I really wanted an intimate relationship with God I realized there were some changes that needed to take place in my life. Little by little, as I spent time with God, I learned to recognize His voice. My first experience hearing from Him was while I was ironing in front of the TV watching my three favorite "Soaps" I loved soap operas and tried to plan my day so I could watch them. As I was ironing I sensed an inner voice saying, "If you don't quit watching this trash you will never grow spiritually." I had no doubt this was God. I was hungry for spiritual growth so I took this seriously and turned off the television immediately. To this day I have never watched another soap opera.

One morning while I was reading my Bible there was a scripture that convicted me of not winning more people to the Lord. It was John 15:1-2 *"I am the true vine, and my Father is the gardener. He cuts off every branch in me that bears no fruit, while every branch that does bear fruit he prunes so that it will be even more fruitful."* (NIV) I couldn't remember the last time I had led someone to accept Jesus. But I reasoned with myself, "I am always around Christians, so how can I witness to anyone?" I felt guilty that I was not bearing fruit, so I prayed and asked God to give me some opportunities to meet people who were unbelievers. The very next week I was asked to become the Director of a new Crisis Pregnancy Center. After I organized the office and recruited volunteer counselors I started doing some counseling myself. Most of the clients were young women between ages of 14 and 20. In the process of getting information from them to fill out the required forms, I could quickly see that most of these girls did not have a relationship with Jesus. They were scared and nervous, which made it easier for me to talk to them and let them know how much God loved them. When my first client prayed with me to accept Jesus into her life I was elated. By the end of the first week there were thirty-five new converts. I was in awe that God would give me this wonderful opportunity.

GOD CARES ABOUT SMALL THINGS

It takes practice to be sure you are hearing God's voice. There were so many times I missed it and later realized God had been speaking to me. When He speaks to us it's always for our good, so we don't want to miss it. I've learned to ask Him to speak to me about all kinds of things, even shopping. It may sound crazy to think that the God of the universe would care about our shopping, but I believe He does. If you care, He cares. If you have an unlimited budget and can buy anything you want whenever you shop, perhaps you don't need any guidance from God about what you buy. I have never been in that position. I usually have a limited amount of money to spend so I ask God's advice about where to go and what to buy. Many times He has led me to places where I got great value for my money. I love that, and I always thank Him for it. There have been times when I tried on a dress or pants suit that really looked great on me, but before I bought them I sensed a check in my spirit, so I put them back. I've learned that the check in my spirit is usually God speaking to me and although it has taken me quite a while to get to this place, I want to obey Him even in the small things. I don't always know the reasons why, but God knows and it's always for my good.

A number of years ago I was asked to speak for a ladies' group, so I prayed for God to give me an outline that would be appropriate for my topic. Immediately in my mind I saw an acrostic of the word "Freedom." It was perfect! He doesn't always answer so quickly, but it's exciting when He does. It makes me feel that He's really interested in what's going on in my life. God speaks to us in many different ways. He may put a thought or a picture into our minds, or He may show us things in a dream or vision like He did for Jacob in the Bible. He also speaks through scripture, circumstances, people, music, poetry, and there have been occasions when He has spoken through angels. The more we learn to recognize His voice the more we will hunger to hear Him again and again.

HEARING AND OBEYING

My husband has been a good example to me of hearing and obeying God's voice. One day he was in the office where we had rented storage space and as he started to leave he sensed God speaking to him to go back into the office and talk to the woman at the desk. She was on the phone, but he could tell she was very troubled about something, so when she hung up the phone he asked if there was anything she would like prayer for. Amid tears she poured out her sad story of how she was now raising her two grandchildren who had been subjected to child pornography by their father and grandfather they were very young. These men were sent to prison and the mother was ordered not to come near them. This loving grandmother didn't earn much money so she struggled financially to support these children, in addition to coping with all the psychological problems they were experiencing. She definitely needed prayer. She also needed someone to encourage her.

When Jud told me the story he asked if I would buy some gifts for the children who were having birthdays the next week. Then at Christmas we bought more gifts and food for the family. We were touched as we observed this godly woman cope with her difficult circumstances. She never lost faith in God and was always appreciative of anything we did for her. It was a blessing to us to be able to assist this family in need and we have developed a lasting friendship. I'm so glad Jud listened and obeyed God's voice.

In 1988 we lived in Lompoc, CA, a place we often said we would like to live forever. It was on the Pacific coast where the weather was perfect, no need for air-conditioners and seldom a need for heat. We attended an exciting church where we had developed some deep friendships. When we first sensed God asking us to move to Corpus Christi, TX to help our family start a Christian television station I thought, "How can I leave our church? I love these people so much!" As we continued receiving confirmation that this is what we were to do, God prepared my heart to leave. By the time we were ready to move, I was so excited about what God had in store for us in Corpus Christi that it wasn't difficult to part with our friends.

THE CALL OF GOD

I've heard many interesting stories about how God called people to various ministries. Some had dreams, some actually heard an audible voice, but most people merely heard that still, small voice speaking to their spirits. In the book of Acts it tells about the Apostle Paul's unusual experience. He was traveling to Damascus when suddenly a bright light flashed from the sky. It was so bright he dropped down onto the ground when he heard an audible voice saying, *"Saul, Saul, why do you persecute me?" "Who are you, Lord?" Saul asked. "I am Jesus, whom you are persecuting," he replied. "Now get up and go into the city, and you will be told what you must do."* Acts 9:4-6 (NIV) At that moment Saul not only became a believer in Jesus Christ, but he received a calling to a world-changing ministry.

My former pastor, Tom Manz, had an interesting experience when God called him to the ministry. He had been a Christian for two years and as it was nearly time for him to complete his tour of duty in the Navy, he had been praying about what God wanted for his future. Shortly after becoming a Christian the men responsible for leading the small group of believers on his ship were transferred. To his amazement he found himself gradually moving into a leadership role teaching Bible studies and discipling new believers. Even though he knew that God had gifted him with ministry abilities he was not certain that it was to be a full-time, life calling.

One night while on a ship off the coast of East Africa, as he was looking out across the dark waters, he saw a vision of himself in a church preaching to people. Then he heard a very clear voice saying, "This is what I want you to do. Preach my Word to the people." Although he was eager to obey this call from God, it was a number of years before he was prepared to fulfill that calling. First he went to Bible College, then he served for a few years as a Youth Pastor. When he thought he was ready to become a pastor and fulfill the call God had given him, God required him to wait another seven years. Finally in 1984 God released him into the ministry for which he had been called.

Together Tom and his wife, Georgiann, started Cornerstone Church in Blue Springs, MO. Today it is a vibrant, exciting church of about 750 people. The vision God showed him has come to pass all because Tom was sensitive and obedient to God's voice. Today he says that the greatest challenge in his spiritual growth and development was learning to wait on the Lord and discover His perfect timing for every season of his life.

GOD CALLS HOUSEWIVES TOO

I remember a time when I sensed that God gave me a definite calling to minister to hurting women. I didn't know in what capacity it would be, but at that time I was the Director of Women's Ministries at our church and I really enjoyed helping the women God brought into my life. I now sensed that God was going to expand my ministry into additional ways of helping women through speaking and writing. I had a strong desire to speak for women's retreats because I had seen so many women's lives changed while attending them. I prayed that the Lord would open the door for me to do this. Finally my opportunity came. A speaker for a retreat had to cancel due to sickness and I was asked to take her place. What a thrill for me! This is what I had been longing for. I was sure this would be the beginning of my speaking for many women's retreats. But I was wrong!

It was fourteen years before I was asked to speak at another retreat. I remembered reading that the Apostle Paul had to wait about 14 years for God to release him into his ministry. I recalled Henry Blackaby saying in the videos of "Experiencing God" that many times when God calls us to a ministry it could be years before we're ready to do it because He has to perfect our character in order to fulfill that calling. Looking back I can see I needed a lot of perfecting. I'm still far from perfect, but through the years God has helped me improve in many areas. Not only has He continued to bring women into my life to encourage or disciple, but He has opened doors for me to do speaking as well as writing.

I recently heard a good analogy about two tomato plants. One was planted in a few inches of soil. It sprouted up quickly and in a short time had tomatoes on it, but because it had such shallow roots it quickly blew over and died. Consequently, it couldn't produce any more tomatoes. The second tomato plant, which was planted in much deeper soil, took longer to sprout. When it finally was able to produce tomatoes it had developed into a strong, healthy plant which produced beautiful fruit for a long time. God knew if I had been released into a speaking ministry after my first retreat I would have been like that first tomato plant. I needed to grow slowly so I could become strong and healthy; so I could produce fruit for a long time. We've all heard the phrase "ready, willing and able." We may think we are ready—we may be willing—but are we able? Only spending time with God will make us able to fulfill the call of God on our lives.

Do you think God would call a woman in her sixties into a speaking ministry? Why not, if He called Moses to speak before Pharaoh at the age of eighty? As I was praying one day I sensed God telling me to start preparing for a speaking ministry. I questioned Him, "Lord, are You sure? You know my age. Who wants to hear a woman my age?" To allay my doubts God led someone in the state of Washington to e-mail me asking if I would speak for their women's retreat in about six months. That did it! I knew I had heard God correctly. He not only arranged for me to have six months to prepare, but they offered to pay me $1,000. What a way to start! For the past two years I have been on five-state speaking circuit for Christian Women's Clubs and it has been very rewarding. Not only have my husband and I met many lovely people in our travels, but a number of women have accepted Jesus as their Savior. God is so good! In one of Oswald Chambers' daily devotions he wrote, "We have to be so one with God that we do not continually need to ask for guidance." In other words, we will get so accustomed to recognizing his leading we will not have any doubt. I remember a song we used to sing in church, "I'll say, yes, Lord, yes." The year I learned that song was a time when I was just learning to obey God about little things as well as big ones. I even had my license plate personalized to read "YES LRD." Some people probably thought I was a little nutty but it spoke to others in a positive way. Once while attending a melodrama, one of the actresses went outside during her break time and spotted my license plate. For some reason it blessed her, so she left a note on my car thanking me.

When we moved from California to Texas, then six years later to Missouri to help start a new church, we were saying "Yes, Lord" because we knew we were hearing God's voice. Last year we made another move to Branson, MO because we felt God leading us to become part of a ministry here. Our obedience usually turned out differently than we expected, but much better than we could have imagined. Ephesians 3:20 tells us that God is able to do *"exceedingly abundantly above all we could ask or think."* That has really been true for us. Hopefully we'll never be so afraid of making a mistake that we miss out on the joy of acting on the voice of the Lord. Gradually we have come to place where we no longer have to ask, "Is that You, God?" We have come to know His voice.

———————— ▼ ————————

CHAPTER 7

WHY CAN'T YOU BE
MORE LIKE ME?

Have you ever wondered why other people aren't more like you? Especially your husband? You like bright colors; he likes drab. You like peppy music; he likes slow. You like to do things spontaneously; he likes to plan everything at least a couple of days in advance. You are kind of messy; he's a neatnik. Does this cause trouble in your relationship? Sure it does!

Perhaps you wish you could have a personality more like somebody else. If you're a quiet, serious person you wish you could be the bubbly, happy-go-lucky, outgoing person like your friend or your husband. If you're the workaholic type that never can sit down and relax, you may want to be like the laid-back, easy-going personality. God created each of us with our own unique personalities for a reason. It wasn't an accident. God knew what He was doing. So I hope this chapter will enable you to understand and enjoy your God-given personality. Once we understand ourselves, then we can begin to understand other people and know how to treat them.

The Apostle Paul said, "*If it is possible, as much as depends on you, live peaceably with all men.*" Romans 12:18 (NIV) I'm sure Paul experienced difficulties in some of his relationships so that's probably why he said, "*If it is possible.*" Living peaceably with everyone is much easier once we understand them. About twenty years ago I first heard Florence Littauer speak on Personalities and it was a real eye-opener for me. Growing up, my four brothers and I were very much alike in our personalities, so I thought the whole world was just like us—bossy, controlling and opinionated. I was so wrong! How I wish I had learned about the differences before I started raising a family. My husband and three daughters were very different from me, but I treated them as though we were all the same personality types.

When I married my husband, Jud, I was forty-eight years old and he was forty-nine. For his fiftieth birthday I planned for months to give him an unforgettable surprise birthday party. I shopped and shopped to find a perfect gift that would please him. When he showed absolutely no excitement about the party or the gift, I was crushed. Since I'm the type who can get excited over something as simple as a new pair of panty hose, I couldn't understand his unemotional response. Once I learned about the different personalities, I discovered that Perfect Melancholies never show enthusiasm about anything. So now I understand that if I ask him how he likes my new dress, which I'm really thrilled with, I have to be satisfied when all he says is, "It's okay." God made him that way so there's no point in my trying to change him. I just love him for who he is. Understanding personalities has helped me so much in all my relationships that I am eager to share what I have learned with anyone who will listen. I really think it should be a required subject in high school and in premarital counseling. It would eliminate a lot of relational problems young people will face in life.

There are many different personality teachings, but this one is easier to understand than some, so hopefully you will enjoy it. Over 2000 years ago Hippocrates gave names to four different personality types and Florence Littauer and her daughter, who I took personality training from, have added descriptive words, plus colors, to each one making them easier to remember. As a rule people are not just one of these personality types. We are usually strong in one and weaker in another, or we may be fifty-fifty between two of them. I hope you will be able to figure out what your personality type is, as well as members of your family or any people with whom you have relationships. (See Personality Profile in the back of the book.)

POPULAR SANGUINE	**POWERFUL CHOLERIC**
PEACEFUL PHLEGMATIC	**PERFECT MELANCHOLY**

POPULAR SANGUINE—YELLOW

This is the "fun" personality. The color yellow is used for them because they are bright, cheery, optimistic people. They're called "The Talkers." They love to talk, they talk a lot and talk loud. You can usually hear them above everyone else in the room. It doesn't bother them if they butt in while you are talking. They are usually waving their hands around or hugging and patting whoever is near them. They like being the center of attention and are the best story-tellers in the world. They can take a dull story and dress it up so you'd never recognize it, but everyone will enjoy it. Folks enjoy ministers who are Popular Sanguines because they preach such "fun" sermons with lots of good stories.

Sanguines love to have a good time and can make fun out of nearly anything. My son-in-law, Chris, is a Popular Sanguine and he's the only person I know who can make changing a baby's poopy diaper a fun thing. He just makes fun out of everything he does. If you are planning a party it's good to invite some of these fun people to liven things up.

They usually have lots of friends and can make a new "best friend" in a matter of seconds. For instance, while standing in line at a grocery store they can strike up a conversation with someone and by the time they reach the checkout counter they are best friends. When I lived in San Antonio, Texas, a friend of mine wanted me to meet her Popular Sanguine neighbor, Bonnie Skinner, so we went to lunch together and had a great time. You always have a good time when you are with Popular Sanguines. As we were leaving Bonnie happened to see a friend of hers on the other side of the restaurant, so she called to her "Jane, come over here and meet my new best friend, Esther."

Sanguines are energized by being with other people. They hate being alone, so it's important when they're looking for employment that they are not going to be stuck in a room with no one to talk to. If you have a Popular Sanguine child the punishment they hate the most is being sent to their room alone. If you punish two children by sending them to the same room, they'll love it. Sanguine children can be very entertaining, but they require a lot of attention and want to be praised for everything they do. If they sing a song for you they want you to clap and tell them how wonderful it was.

Popular Sanguines are very charming, in addition to being born sales people. So be on your guard or they may talk you into buying something you never intended to buy. Their charm also helps them get hired for jobs easily. My Sanguine daughter, Debbe, went to a classy ladies' fitness center to apply for a job and before she told the woman at the front desk why she was there, the woman (who turned out to be the manager) showed her around the gym. By the time they finished the tour they had become "best friends," so when Debbe asked about the position that was available, the woman hired her on the spot without even asking her to fill our a job application. Because of their charm Sanguines can get hired for jobs easily, but if it doesn't turn out to be a fun job they'll get bored and move on to something else.

When someone is asking for volunteers, Sanguines will be the first to respond because they want people to like them. However, since they are not organized people they don't usually carry a calendar or pen in their purses to write down what they volunteered for. Consequently, they don't remember when, where or what they volunteered for. It's good to remember this if you are recruiting people to help with a project. If you know they are Popular Sanguines you might want to give them a call to remind them.

Popular Sanguines tend to be rather messy but if they know you are coming to their house they want things to look good because your approval is very important to them. They will shove things into closets, drawers, or the bedroom so the living room will be all tidied up when you arrive. If you notice the bedroom door is closed, don't go there! I recently saw a program on television where people were hired to organize someone's home. The family being interviewed must have been Sanguines because they said when company was coming they would pile things into laundry baskets and hide them in the bedroom till their guests departed. They paid big bucks for these organizers to create a place for everything so their house wouldn't be such a mess, but I couldn't help but wonder how long it would stay organized.

Sanguines are spontaneous. They like to do things on the spur of the moment. They can be on their way to a meeting but if you invite them to go to lunch at a fun place, they're ready to go. Forget the meeting! They also love to go shopping, but since they don't usually balance their checkbooks they have no idea how much money is in their bank account. That doesn't stop them if they find a pretty dress or classy looking pair of shoes on sale. They'll usually find a way to justify buying things even when they shouldn't. Looking pretty is important to them.

Popular Sanguines are very artistic—great at crafts. However, they get bored easily so if a project takes too long they'll quit. Consequently they often have a lot of unfinished projects stored in the basement or garage. I can relate to this because I am partly Popular Sanguine. A number of years ago everyone was into making appliquéd t-shirts made with fabric designs, outlined with glue and glitter. At Christmastime I decided to make t-shirts for Christmas gifts. I bought the cardboard shirt forms, various holiday printed fabrics, glue, glitter and some sparkly stones for decoration. I made t-shirts for all the females in our family from my two-year-old granddaughter to my eighty-eight-year-old mother-in-law. I loved having everyone ooh and aah about how darling the shirts were, but I was getting bored so when Christmas was over I never wanted to make another t-shirt for the rest of my life.

PERFECT MELANCHOLY—BLUE

You will notice on the personality diagram Popular Sanguine and Perfect Melancholy are opposite each other. That's because they are also opposite in personality. The Sanguines talk a lot and talk loud, but the Perfect Melancholies don't talk much and they're quiet. The color blue is appropriate for them because they sometimes look sad. They don't smile much. They're very serious people—called "The Thinkers." They like everything to be perfect and their motto is "If it's worth doing, it's doing right."

Melancholies don't enjoy being around a lot of people; they enjoy their own quiet space. They make good CPAs because they enjoy details and working alone. They <u>always</u> balance their checkbooks and don't spend money, or do anything else, impulsively. They like to plan ahead for everything. If you want to go to lunch with a Perfect Melancholy it's best to give them at least 24 hours notice so they can put it on their "to-do" list.

My husband, Jud, a Perfect Melancholy, keeps a list in his pocket at all times of what he's planning to do for the next couple of days. If I ask him to do something that isn't on his list, it messes up his day. I must admit, however, through the years he has become much more flexible.

Where the Popular Sanguines are messy, the Perfect Melancholies are tidy and neat about nearly everything. Many couples are this combination so it's quite an adjustment for them. Melancholies like their closets and dresser drawers to be in perfect order with every shirt hung in the same direction on the same kind of hangers. All the dress shirts are together as well as the sport shirts and slacks. You would never find a pair of slacks mixed in with the shirts or one shirt facing a different direction than the others. Jud likes all his socks to be the same brand and folded all the same way. Since he's retired he wears a lot of white socks with his athletic shoes, and if he gets a stain on a sock he uses a black magic marker to put a big "W" on the sock identifying it as a "Work Sock."

We have moved twelve times during our marriage and I have learned not to ask Jud help me hang pictures if I'm in a hurry. He is such a perfectionist it takes him twice as long as if I did it myself. He has to measure down from the ceiling, up from the floor, and in from both sides of the wall. Then he uses a pencil, not a pen, to put an "X" in the exact spot where the nail should go. He selects the right size nail for the picture and when he hangs the picture, it is done perfectly. I'm too impatient for that. When I hang pictures I whack a nail in, hang the picture, then stand back and take a look. If it's not just right I take the picture down, pull out the nail, and whack another one in a different spot. Sometimes I have three or four holes in the wall but I figure, "Who looks under the pictures?" However, when we move Jud has to patch up all those holes in the wall.

Perfect Melancholies do not want a lot of "new best friends" like the Popular Sanguines. They prefer one or two faithful, loyal friends.

POWERFUL CHOLERIC—RED

If you have ever attended an art class you probably learned that the color red denotes action. That's the perfect color for the Powerful Choleric because they are active, busy people. They're called "The Doers." The Nike ad "Just Do It!" must have been meant for them. They can accomplish more work than any other personality type. Usually Cholerics are presidents of organizations or big companies due to their leadership ability. Because they enjoy working so much, many of them tend to become workaholics. Although they enjoy working they want you to notice what they do and tell them how much you appreciate them. If you have Powerful Choleric children it's good to praise them when you've given them a job to do. They thrive on that!

Recently my husband and I were in a Starbucks in another town when a woman came in and started picking up all the newspapers, putting them in the magazine rack, wiping all the tables and straightening the chairs. Jud asked her "Do you work here?" She replied "No, I just like to help tidy it up." You could tell by the way she entered the room and took charge, she was definitely a Powerful Choleric.

Cholerics tend to be impatient people. The next time you're standing in a long line anywhere, take a look at the people who are waiting. You'll be able to spot the Cholerics. They're fidgeting, looking at their watches, rolling their eyes, and might even express their frustration about the wait.

Powerful Cholerics want things done their way and want them done "right now." Since they are born with the ability to be leaders they can be very controlling and bossy. This is my personality so I know from my own experience that we need God's help to change us from these offensive ways. Cholerics are also known to say things in a harsh, tactless way many times, which hurts people's feelings. Before God changed me I had to do a lot of apologizing.

Powerful Cholerics can make decisions quickly and are usually right, which is good in the business world, but if confronted with something they've done wrong, they have a hard time admitting their error or saying "I'm sorry." You can imagine the problems a married couple would have if they were both Powerful Cholerics. They both want to be boss, both think they are right, and neither one ever wants to say "I'm sorry." If they can learn to resolve these issues they can be a dynamite couple because they are both leaders and hard workers. They have a lot of self confidence and are usually willing to try new things, even if they are difficult.

One of the Choleric's main weakness is they don't have much tolerance for other people's weaknesses. They can't see their own weaknesses but they can spot them in other people and it's annoying to them. They also are not compassionate, merciful people. I once took a spiritual gifts test and in the area of "Mercy" I scored zero. Fortunately, God can change us and help us to become more tender-hearted.

PEACEFUL PHLEGMATIC—GREEN

Think of sitting in a park during Springtime enjoying the beauty of all the green trees and grass. Isn't it a peaceful feeling? That's why green is a good color for the Peaceful Phlegmatics. They are peaceful people with low-energy. They don't want to be busy like the Powerful Cholerics, the "Doers," who are always working. They'd much rather watch. Therefore, they're called "The Watchers." They would always rather rest than work. I found a greeting card at the Hallmark store with a picture of an obviously Phlegmatic woman lying in a hammock saying, "How wonderful it is to do nothing, and rest afterwards."

Peaceful Phlegmatics are the kindest, sweetest people you will ever meet. They make good school principals because they don't offend the parents, teachers, or students. They don't offend anyone! They're contented people who don't have a need to change anyone or anything, so they're enjoyable to be around. They make good employees because they get along with everyone and stay on their jobs a long time. Phlegmatics do not like to make decisions, even small ones. If asked, "Would you like coffee or tea?" they usually reply something liked, Either one…. whatever's easy … I don't care."

Many Peaceful Phlegmatics have jobs that do not necessarily suit their personality type, but if they make up their minds to do it, they can. For instance, a number of United States presidents have been Peaceful Phlegmatic men, and that's not exactly the kind of position you would expect for a person who can't make decisions, and loves to rest. They're rather like chameleons who can change their color to fit in with their surroundings. Phlegmatics can do whatever is necessary on their job, but then when they come home they revert back to their own personality.

Once I did a Personality teaching for the youth of our church and afterwards the Youth Pastor's wife said, "Now I understand my husband. He can go all day having a blast with the kids, but then when he comes home he just wants to sit in his Lazy Boy talking to no one, just resting. He's being a combination of Popular Sanguine and Powerful Choleric during the day, but at home he reverts back to his true Phlegmatic personality."

They also have a hard time saying no. Consequently, they often buy things from door to door salesmen which they have no use for. They also agree to do jobs at their church or for their children's sports activities, which cause them to be much too busy. For low energy people, being too busy is not good, and can cause them to become depressed. My daughter, Becky, has recently experienced this. She's so sweet that she agrees to do things instead of speaking up and saying she's too busy. Then she can't handle everything she has committed to. She finds there is no time for herself, no time to relax, nothing but work, work, work. For a low-energy person this can be a real problem. Recently she came to a place where she just couldn't take the pressure and had to get away from everything for about a week. After that she was fine but she learned through that experience to say no sometimes instead of getting overloaded.

Because Peaceful Phlegmatics are so "nice," sometimes people take advantage of them. I have a story like that about two of my grandsons, Michael and Brandon, when they were little. Michael is a combination Powerful Choleric and Perfect Melancholy (he wants everything done his way and done right), and his younger brother, Brandon is mostly Peaceful Phlegmatic. Prior to their visit my husband put two suckers, one red and one green, on the counter in the bathroom knowing the boys would find them. Sure enough, Michael found them. He came out of the bathroom saying "Look, Brandon, suckers," as he handed the green one to him. I said "Wait a minute, why don't you ask Brandon which one he would like?" Michael begrudgingly asked "Brandon, which one would you like?" Brandon, in a typical Phlegmatic response replied, "I would like whichever one Michael would like to give me."

This has been just a thumb-nail sketch of the four basic personality types. I hope you have been able to identify with one or more of them. The purpose of learning about the different personality types is not so we can say, "I'm a Powerful Choleric so I can be bossy." Or "I'm 'The Talker'" so you just have to put up with my talking too much." No, once we discover our true personalities we learn that we all have some areas in which to improve. Sometimes, as in my case, we need God's help in order to change.

In school most of us learned the Golden Rule "Do unto others as you would have them do unto you." However, in order to get along better with other people it would be better to "Do unto others as THEY would have YOU do unto THEM." If we learn to treat people the way they want to be treated according to their personalities, relationships will begin to improve. I've experienced this in my own life.

When people don't understand the Personalities, they don't realize what their spouses need from them. Many marriages have been saved just by learning about each other's personality type. This works in all relationships, not just marriages. If you are interested in learning more about personality types there are a number of books listed in "Suggested Reading" in the back of this book. There is also a Personality Profile which will help you determine your own personality type.

CHAPTER 8

▼

IT'S NOT ABOUT ME!

Today's Society teaches us to look out for Number One. It's all about us! But the Bible teaches us that it's about others, not us. In Ephesians 2:10 (Living) it tells us that God planned that we should spend our lives helping others. The natural man is self-serving, but when we become Christians the spiritual man develops a desire to serve others instead of always thinking first of ourselves. The more we allow the Holy Spirit to rule in our lives the more we desire to be like Jesus who was the model servant. *"... the Son of Man did not come to be served, but to serve, ..."* Matthew 20:28 (NKJ)

Serving others means more than just taking care of our families. That's easy to do because we care so much about them and we know it's our responsibility. God's plan for us is to reach out to people in need, sometimes people we don't even know or like. They might be people who are not easy to love. You may be thinking, "I'd be glad to serve people in need if I knew someone like that." If we don't know anyone, all we have to do is ask God to present some opportunities to us. Believe me, He'll do it, so when you ask, you'd better be serious about it.

Oswald Chambers wrote in one of his devotionals "If we are devoted to the cause of humanity, we shall soon be crushed and broken hearted, for we shall often meet with more ingratitude from men than we would from a dog; but if our motive is love to God, no ingratitude can hinder us from serving our fellow man." To be a good servant we have to change our thinking. We must realize life is not all about us. The Bible teaches us to prefer others above ourselves. That's hard to do.

Most of us take for granted all the conveniences that make our lives so easy and enjoyable, e.g. getting into a nice car parked in a warm garage when it's wintertime. We never think about the person who has no garage, or perhaps who has no car and has to rely on public transportation. Do we ever think about offering that person a ride? No, it might delay us a few minutes. What about the young mother who brings her three or four small children to church every Sunday. Do we ever inquire about her circumstances. Does she have a husband? Does she have anyone to give her a break from caring for those children? Could she use a little help with laundry, cooking or cleaning? What about the single person? A divorcee, a widow or widower, or someone who has never married? Do we ever think how lonely it must be for them to eat alone night after night? Do we invite them to our home for a meal? What about that person who needs to be taken to a hospital for dialysis on a regular basis? Would they enjoy someone taking them to give them a little company? There are all kinds of ways we can serve people. Rick Warren, in *The Purpose Driven Life,* wrote "When we stop focusing on our own needs, we become aware of the needs of others." Jesus was a good example of a true servant, one we can pattern our lives after.

SERVANTS' HEARTS

Joe and Dee Vincent, some friends of ours who live in Hot Springs Village, Arkansas were blessed by a woman God spoke to about serving others. Joe was diagnosed with stomach cancer and after extensive surgery went through a long struggle with chemotherapy treatments. During this time a friend volunteered to clean their house every week. She definitely wasn't thinking about herself. She had a servant's heart.

A couple who have servants' hearts are Doug and Pam Bartow. About five years ago God gave Doug a vision of a Food Ministry He wanted them to start. They were so confident they had heard from the Lord, Doug quit his lucrative job in the business world and, with no visible means of support, they started "Living Bread Ministries." It was a huge leap of faith. They had no regular paycheck for the first 18 months. However, God supplied all their needs and today the food ministry is providing food to approximately 300 families each week. It has grown immensely since its inception, and many people's live have been blessed because of the Bartows' willingness to be God's servants.

BLESS AND BE BLESSED

A few years ago I received a flyer from the local Christian book store advertising a book entitled, "A Cup of Hope" by Emily Barnes. I sensed God telling me I was supposed to buy that book, so I did. As I browsed through it I wondered why God wanted me to buy this particular book, but as I read how Emily was going through a battle with cancer I knew the answer. I was to read it to an elderly friend named Annie who was also struggling with cancer. I went to her house two or three days a week and read only one chapter at a time, then we would discuss it. The book was just what the title said, "A Cup of Hope." Annie and Emily were going through exactly the same things. Emily always offered hope and encouragement so Annie enjoyed every word I read to her. My strong, Choleric personality does not enjoy being around sick people but God enabled me to enjoy reading to Annie. I know she was blessed by my reading to her, but I think I was the one who received the most blessing. I never heard a negative word from her—only words of hope. Although Annie passed away, she never gave up hope right until the end. I'll always be thankful God gave me the opportunity to be a servant to Annie.

In the Bible the book of Ruth is a story about a young Moabite woman who willingly left her homeland to go to Bethlehem and care for her Jewish mother-in-law, Naomi. She truly had a servant's heart. I have always loved this story but I had no idea how meaningful it would become in my own life.

Twelve years ago Jud and I invited his mother, Winifred, to come live with us. She was eighty-three and in good health, but she lived alone in Iowa where the weather was severe in the wintertime. We thought it would be good for her to be in sunny San Antonio, Texas. She was very active and fun to be with, so I was looking forward to having her with us. She was delighted at the thought of coming, although a little sad to leave her lifelong friends. Three months after she came to live with us she had a major heart attack. The cardiologist scheduled her for a quadruple bypass. On Sunday prior to her surgery our pastor preached a sermon from the book of Ruth. During his sermon I sensed God asking me if I would be willing to be a "Ruth" to my mother-in-law. I silently said "Yes." On the day prior to her surgery I attended a women's prayer meeting. At the beginning of the meeting the leader said, "I don't know what this means, but I sense that God is speaking to one of you ladies about being a "Ruth" to someone." I'm sure no one else understood what she was talking about, but to me this was confirmation of what God had spoken to me.

Winifred came through the surgery with flying colors and after five days was released to come home. I then became her nurse, something I had never aspired to be. Many young girls dream of growing up to be a nurse, but not me. However, Winifred needed a nurse, and I was the only one available whether I liked it or not. She had two long incisions in her left leg as well as a huge one down the middle of her chest which had to be bathed twice a day. I wondered how I could do this. I have learned that whenever God asks us to do something He enables us to do it. This was no exception. Before long I could clean those incisions without feeling squeamish at all. He helped me to lovingly serve her as long as she needed me. I think He must have helped her too, because although she was in a great deal of pain she was a very sweet, appreciative patient. She lived with us for seven years before going to a Health Care facility and recently went on to heaven to be with Jesus. I don't know if I served my mother-in-law as well as Ruth in the Bible, but during the years she lived with us God taught me a great deal about having a servant's heart.

I recall a Christmas when we shared our home with a young woman and her six children whose husband was in prison. Another time we invited a woman to stay with us for six weeks when she didn't have a place to live. And there was a time when God prompted me to speak to a black woman in the lobby of our church. In a matter of seconds she was crying and telling me her story, which she continued after church when we took her to lunch. There's no end to the opportunities God will bring our way if we are willing to be servants. When we bless others, we are blessed in return.

I Peter 4:16 (NIV) says *"Each one should use whatever gift he has received to serve others, faithfully administering God's grace in its various forms.* Have you ever thought about what gifts God has given you that can be used to serve others? We all have them whether we recognize them or not. If you are naturally a great cook, that's a gift, and it can be used to serve others. If God has given you a talent to be a musician, poet, seamstress, gardener, or anything that can be useful to serve others, ask Him who you can bless by being a servant to them. If we want to be like Jesus, we must quit thinking of ourselves first and develop a genuine interest in serving others. When we do good things to help people the Bible says we're doing it unto God. *"'I tell you the truth, whatever you did for one of the least of these brothers of mine, you did for me.'"* Mat. 25:34 (NIV) After all, it's not about us, it's about Him.

▼

CHAPTER 9

LAUGH, AND LIVE LONGER!

"Learn the sweet magic of a cheerful face."

Oliver Wendell Holmes

This chapter is about humor. I'm not an especially funny person but I'm learning to laugh more as I get older. Doctors say laughter is healthy for us. *"A cheerful heart does good like medicine, but a broken spirit makes one sick."* Proverbs 17:22 (TLB) As we grow older there are many things that take place in our bodies and minds that we may not like. We can get cranky, we can get depressed, we can spend a lot of money trying to prevent these things from happening, or we can just accept them as part of the aging process that happens to everybody and learn to laugh about them. There's a group of ladies I used to go to lunch with once a month who, like me, were experiencing some of these things. When we got together we laughed about everything. Observers probably thought we were a little tipsy, but we weren't. We had simply learned how to laugh about things instead of letting them stress us.

"Beautiful young people are accidents of nature, but beautiful old people are works of art." (Anonymous)

I think learning to laugh at ourselves is part of becoming beautiful old people.

VANITY, VANITY!

I remember the day I had to start wearing reading glasses. It was in the early seventies when glasses were not as attractive as they are today, so I wasn't very happy about wearing them. I would put them on to read something and very quickly take them off. In a few years I noticed I wasn't able to read the speedometer or a map while driving. It was a safety hazard to dig my glasses out of my purse while driving, so my only option was to start wearing the glasses whenever I was in the car. Soon I was wearing them full-time everywhere, and by now it was worse. I needed bifocals! Horrors! Now I not only had to wear glasses that made me feel ugly, but they had a noticeable line right across the middle of the lenses.

My vanity led me to experimenting with contacts. For people who needed bifocals they informed me they used what was called monovision.... one eye for distance and the other for reading. I wanted so much to wear contacts but apparently I was allergic to the material used in the contacts. They made my eyes all red and puffy, so I finally gave in to wearing the bifocals. Before long they didn't bother me at all. I guess one of the things we have to accept as we age is that vanity should not control our lives.

In Marjorie Holmes' book *Lord, Let Me Love,* she wrote:

> "Oh, God, dear God, I'm showing my age. I'm not young and beautiful any more, the way my heart imagines. When I look in the mirror I could cry. For I look just what I am—a woman growing older. And I protest it, Lord. Perhaps foolishly, I am stricken. "Vanity, vanity, all is vanity," the Bible says. Dear God, if this be vanity, let me use it to some good purpose. Let it inspire me to keep my body strong and well and agile, the way you made it in the beginning. May it help me to stay as attractive as possible for as long as possible—out of concern for other people as well as myself. For you, who made women, also know that when we feel attractive we're a lot easier to live with. But oh, God, whatever happens to my face and body, keep me always supple in spirit, resilient to new ideas, beautiful in the things I say and do. If I must "show my age" let it be in some deeper dimension of beauty that is ageless and eternal, and can only come from you. Don't let me be so afraid of aging, God. Let me rejoice and reach out to be replenished; I know that each day I can be reborn into strength and beauty through you."

LEARNING TO LAUGH

"A happy face means a glad heart; a sad face means a breaking heart." Proverbs 15:13(TLB) Have you ever noticed how many older women look unhappy? They probably have not learned to laugh at the changes taking place in them. They

don't have a happy face because they don't have a glad heart. They may not have much hope for what's ahead. Frank Lloyd Wright once said, "The present is the ever-moving shadow that divides yesterday from tomorrow. In that lies hope. Our bodies and minds may be changing as we age but it doesn't have to destroy our hope."

Some of the things I am going to share with you are things that troubled me at first, but I gradually found that laughing about them made me feel much better.

"You don't stop laughing because you grow old; you grow old because you stop laughing." (Anonymous)

Hair Color: In my younger days my red hair was my best feature, but as I grew older my once beautiful red hair started looking faded. Occasionally white hairs appeared here and there. I thought, "No problem! I'll just have my hair dresser put a little color on it." As the years have passed it has become necessary to color it more frequently. In fact, now I have to do it every three weeks. For some reasons redheads don't turn salt and pepper, then into a beautiful white. They just get more faded. That's not for me. I like color. When I go to the beauty shop for a touch-up I leave feeling beautiful. That's the way we all want to feel, isn't it?

Wrinkles: The first time a wrinkle appeared I thought I had smeared makeup on my face, but when I rubbed it, it didn't disappear. That was the first of many. I must admit, it has been difficult sometimes to laugh when I try to put on lip liner or eye liner and it just accentuates the wrinkles. Sometimes when I finish putting on my makeup I look in the mirror and think, "Hmm, not bad!" but then I put on my glasses. I have learned that using a good-quality moisture cream helps in addition to staying out of the sun. (Tanning booths will age us before our time.) We have to do whatever we can to make our skin look good. For some of us it takes a lot of effort. Have you ever seen one of those greeting cards with a terribly wrinkled lady who says, "If I had known I was going to live so long, I'd have taken better care of myself"? It's meant to be funny but it is something to think about. Not long after I noticed wrinkles appearing on my face, I began to notice them on our arms also. Years ago I remember not wanting to wear sleeveless blouses because my arms were too fat, but now instead of being fat they are too wrinkled, so I still don't wear sleeveless blouses. I've gradually learned to laugh about my "turkey" arms but I still don't like to display them in public.

Facial Hair: I used to laugh at my elderly mother-in-law's occasional chin whiskers until one day I discovered a few on my own chin. Then I began to notice I had a blonde mustache and sort of a peach-fuzz growing on my cheeks. Now in my five-strength mirror I carefully look over my face every few days and trim off all unwanted hair (I don't shave though.) I recently saw a woman in a restaurant who actually had a dark beard. It made me thankful that my facial hair was blonde.

Failing Memory: Forgetting things can be funny, annoying and sometimes embarrassing. When you want to introduce your best friend and can't remember her name, that's definitely embarrassing. That's happened to me so many times I now tell people ahead of time, "If I don't introduce you it's because I have either forgotten their name or yours."

Forgetting where I park my car is a frequent problem. Sometimes I not only forget where it is in the parking lot, but which parking lot. Florence Littauer tells a story of losing her car in a five-story parking garage. She not only forgot which level she parked on, but she couldn't remember which car she drove.

One day after I finished helping my daughter move to her new house, I was in my car on my way home when I noticed I had forgotten my cell phone. I went back to her house but she had already left. Fortunately my cell phone was on the front porch. When I got out to pick up the phone I left the car running. Apparently I bumped the lock on the door as I got out and the wind blew the car door shut. There I was locked out of my car, which was running. Fortunately I now had my cell phone so I called my husband and asked him to come to my rescue. It definitely didn't make his day to drive twenty-five miles to unlock my car. I wanted to laugh but I could tell he didn't see any humor in it. (Perfect Melancholies don't laugh much.) My husband has also had a few memory problems. (I didn't remind him of this, of course.) Once when we were ready to leave for a cross-country driving vacation he forgot where he had hidden our Travelers' checks. He finally decided they must be in one of the suitcases that were already packed so we would find them when we unpacked at the first destination. Not true. We didn't find them until years later when we moved to another house. Fortunately the company issued us new Travelers' checks.

Other things I've learned to laugh about are:

- Putting ice cream in the fridge instead of the freezer

- Seeing a bug crawl up the wall that turned out to be a "floater"

- Falling asleep in church

- Having to buy larger purses to accommodate my pill box

- Asking for senior discounts

- Having grocery baggers ask if they may carry my groceries

- Trying to get the key out of the ignition before I put it into "park"

- LA-Z-BOY becoming my favorite piece of furniture
- Trying to make thinning hair look thick
- Needing a handle to get out of the bathtub
- Asking people to speak louder on the telephone
- Preferring comfortable shoes rather than stylish ones
- Allowing more time to make myself look presentable
- Trying to pay a Casual Corner bill at a Kohl's store
- Forgetting to put sugar in a chocolate pie

Can you relate to any of these things? Or are you too young? Think of some of the things that have happed to you as you've grown older. Do they annoy you or have you learned to laugh about them?

HUMOROUS E-MAILS

Do you have friends that send you humorous e-mails? I do. I have a lot of them. More than I really want. I delete some of them but I have saved a few. Here's one of them.

PERKS OF BEING OVER 50

Kidnappers are not very interested in you.

In a hostage situation you are likely to be released first.

No one expects you to run—anywhere.

People call at 9 PM and ask, "Did I wake you?"

There is nothing left to learn the hard way.

Things you buy now won't wear out.

You can live without sex but not your glasses.

You no longer think of speed limits as a challenge.

You quit trying to hold your stomach in no matter who walks into the room.

Your eyes won't get much worse.

Your secrets are safe with your friends because they can't remember them either.

You know you're getting older when:

Your children begin to look middle-aged.

You look forward to a dull evening at home.

You've got too much room in the house, but not enough in the medicine cabinet.

Your favorite part of the newspaper is "Twenty-five Years Ago."

You know all the answers but nobody asks the questions.

The gray-haired man you help across the street is your husband.

You feel like the morning after but you haven't been anywhere.

LET'S GET SERIOUS

We all need to laugh occasionally, but let's get serious for a few moments. Sometimes laughter is a cover-up. Many comedians learned to be funny to cover the pain they felt inside. We don't want our laughter to be a cover-up for pain within us. As we age it's easy to start feeling unimportant.... like a nobody. Our older years should be the time we feel best about ourselves. If you are one of those people who is feeling like you're a nobody because you're not young any longer, I'd like to share with you some scriptures from the Bible which will help you know how important you are to God.

> **You are a child of God.** John 1:12 (NKJ) *"But as many as received Him, to them He gave the right to become children God, even to those who believe in His name."*
> **You are a co-heir with Christ.** Romans 8:16-17 (NKJ) *"The Spirit Himself bears witness with our spirit that we are children of God, and if children, then heirs—heirs of God and joint heirs with Christ,"*
> **You are Christ's friends.** John 15:15 (NKJ) *"No longer do I call you servants, for a servant does not know what his master is doing; but I have called you friends …"*
> **God knew you before you were ever conceived.** Jeremiah 1:5 (NKJ) "Before I formed you in the womb I knew you."
> **You were not a mistake; all your days were written in His book.** Psalm 139:15-16 *(NKJ) "My frame was not hidden from You, When I was made in secret, And skillfully wrought in the lowest parts of the earth. Your eyes saw my*

substance, being yet unformed. And in Your book they all were written, the days fashioned for me, when as yet there were none of them."

God loves you because you are His child and He is your Father. 1 John 3:1 (NKJ) *Behold what manner of love the Father has bestowed on us, that we should be called children of God!"*

God will always love you. Jeremiah 31:3 (NKJ) *"Yes, I have loved you with an everlasting love;"*

God thinks about you. Psalm 139:17-18 (NKJ) *"How precious also are Your thoughts to me, O God! How great is the sum of them! If I should count them, they would be more in number than the sand;"*

God has good plans for your future. Jeremiah 29:11 (NKJ) *"For I know the thoughts that I think toward you, says the LORD, thoughts of peace and not of evil, to give you a future and a hope".*

God loves you so much He gave His only Son to die that you might live. John 3:16 (NKJ) *"For God so loved the world that He gave His only begotten Son, that whoever believes in Him should not perish but have everlasting life."*

Now do you see how special you are? No matter what your age, your looks, your circumstances, God loves you more than you can imagine and He has many wonderful things in store for you. In her book *Discipline of the Beautiful Woman* Anne Ortlund wrote about the Proverbs 31 woman. She said that as she was studying this passage of scripture she noticed there were twenty-two verses describing this woman's kindness, godliness, hard work, loving relationships— and only one verse out of the twenty-two describing how she looked, although she was very apparently attractive. Seeing this kind of proportion, she told God she wanted to give 1/22 of her time to making herself as outwardly beautiful as she could, and all the rest of her time to becoming wise, kind, godly, hard-working, and the rest. I think that's a good prayer for all of us.

Growing older doesn't happen all of a sudden. It happens gradually and we can enjoy every part of the journey if we will just learn to laugh about things that occur along the way.

CHAPTER 10

▼

FRIENDS ARE A TREASURE!

"Friends are those rare souls who ask how you are, and then wait
to hear the answer."

By Ed Cunningham

Are you one of those people who say, "I wish I had some close friends."? Proverbs 18:24 says *"A man that hath friends must show himself friendly."* (KJV) Dale Carnegie said, "You can make more friends in two months by becoming interested in other people than you can in two years by trying to get other people interested in you." Once we find some good friends we need to work at preserving those friendships. As we get older friendships become more important so we need to keep them alive and well. It doesn't just happen, it takes some effort.

If I were to ask twenty women, "How would you define a friend?" there would probably be twenty different answers, such as:

Someone who loves me

Someone who brings me chicken soup when I'm sick

Someone who likes to hang out with me no matter what we're doing

Someone who will go dress shopping with me and help select something that makes me look great

Someone who builds my confidence, encourages me and tells me, "You can do it."

Someone who sees my faults but likes me anyway

Someone who prays with me when I have a problem

Someone who will watch my kids for a weekend to give me a break

Notice that these responses are all about what a friend would do for us. Friendship is much more than this, it's a two-way street. Are we willing to do or be all of these things for our friends? Having a close friend is a wonderful blessing. Most of us only have a few throughout our lifetimes, but many casual friends. Samuel Johnson once said, "A man, sir, should keep his friendships in a state of constant repair."

NURTURING FRIENDSHIPS

Friendships, like marriages, don't survive without some effort. If we're too busy to spend any time with our friends the relationships will flounder. If you have too many "best friends" there's no way you can spend time with them all, but for the select few that you value most highly, here are a few suggestions for keeping your friendship alive.

1. Send an occasional greeting card, either from a card shop or homemade.

2. Invite them to your home for lunch or dinner, or maybe coffee in the morning. Instead of saying, "Come by sometime and we'll have lunch"—we need to make it happen.

3. When we're on a trip, it's nice to bring them a small gift to let them know we were thinking of them, something that shows our personal interest, not a souvenir type gift.

4. Call them often just to say "Hi" and find out how they're doing. Ask if they have any prayer needs, then be sure to pray for them.

5. If our friend is single and we're married, we could make a little extra dinner to take to them. It's no fun cooking for one. Many singles live on TV dinners or fast food because they don't want to cook.

6. Take an interest in their families or pets.

7. Invite them to a movie or shopping. If we're on a limited budget we could rent a movie to watch together.

8. If they are sick, take a meal or soup and offer to help around their house. If they have children we could take them with us for a while to give our friend some rest.

9. Show them love in any way we can.

I came across some anonymous quotes on friendship that are good to ponder:

> **"Real friends are those who, when you've made a fool of yourself don't feel you've done a permanent job."**
> **"Some men have their first dollar. The man who is really rich is the one who still has his first friend."**
> **"Friendship is like a bank account: you can't continue to draw on it without making deposits"**
> **"A person can hear, but a friend listens for the meaning."**

MY SPECIAL FRIEND

Friends are many things. They do nice things for you. They make you feel good about yourself. They enjoy spending time with you. They like you for who you are. They are willing to tell you things about yourself you need to know, even though you may not want to hear them.

About fourteen years ago when I was working at a Crisis Pregnancy Center in San Antonio, Texas, I met a woman named Beth who initiated the start of a friendship between us by asking me to be her prayer partner. We became close friends, the kind you can tell your innermost thoughts to without fear of destroying your friendship. I especially remember one incident when she gave me some very wise advice. My mother-in-law, Win, who was living with us, was a fearful person who worried about everything. This particular day she was so worried about my husband, Jud, not getting home exactly when expected that she said, "What if he's been killed?" It really bugged me that she was always such a worry-wart and this time I blew up. My words to her were not very gentle; in fact, I was quite harsh.

It happened to be my day to go to Beth's to pray together so I was glad for an excuse to get out of the house. When I arrived at Beth's house I blurted out the story about my mother-in-law. Instead of telling me I was justified in being upset with Win, Beth looked me right in the eye and asked, "Have you ever been afraid?" I thought for a second before replying "No, I don't think so." "Well then" she continued, "you have no idea what it's like to be afraid." She then shared with me that for many years she had been in bondage to fear, but God had completely delivered her from it. It really opened my eyes and I felt ashamed of myself. I'm so glad she didn't agree with me, but lovingly told me I was wrong. From that moment on I had a deeper understanding for Win, as well as for other people who are fearful.

Another incident I recall about Beth is the time she told me something I had said offended her. It took courage for her to confront me because Beth's personality is gentle and kind, not wanting to hurt anyone's feelings, but she cared enough about our friendship that she was willing to let me know I had offended her. This is a true friend. Although we now live in different states and only see each other every other year we still have a close friendship.

MY VERY BEST FRIEND

Growing up in the church we often sang a hymn, *What a Friend We Have in Jesus*. As a child I wasn't able to relate to Jesus as my friend. I thought friends were children who played games, cut out paper dolls, or built snowmen with me. Jesus didn't do any of these things. I couldn't see Him, touch Him or talk to Him, so how could He be my friend?

Now, many years later, I understand how Jesus can be my very best friend. He is always there when I need Him. He comforts me when I am grieving. He makes me feel loved when I feel unlovable. He encourages me when I feel inadequate. He forgives me when I mess up. I could go on and on telling you all the attributes of this wonderful friend.

BEING FRIENDS WITH GOD

We all know that God loves us but does He know that we love Him? Have we developed a friendship with Him? It's not hard to develop a friendship with God. He's not far away, like many people think. He's with us every moment. He's not scary or mean. He's loving and kind. He's not condemning, waiting to punish us. He's forgiving. We can develop a beautiful relationship that will last forever by doing things like spending time with Him; letting Him talk to us, letting Him know how much we appreciate all the wonderful things He does for us, and doing anything He asks us to.

Many people have a friendship with God until something bad happens in their lives like losing a loved one, a job or health. Then they blame God and don't want to be friends anymore. That's not true friendship. Proverbs 17:17 (NKJ) says "*A friend loves at all times.*" God loves us and He never causes bad things to happen to us. There is no friend on earth that could ever love us as much as God does. Even when we turn away from Him temporarily, He keeps right on loving us, wanting us to come back to Him.

FRIENDS HELP FRIENDS

There are some good examples of friendships in the Bible. One of them is between David before he became king and Jonathan, the son of King Saul. This story is found In 1 Samuel, Chapters 18–20. From the moment they met David and Jonathan had a love for each other that developed into a very special friendship. After David became so popular among the Israelites for killing the giant, Goliath, King Saul became very jealous of him and tried to kill him a number of times. Jonathan tried to convince is father not to kill him and then later helped David escape when it was evident his life was in imminent danger. Their friendship continued even after Jonathan's death when David brought Jonathan's crippled son, Mephibosheth, to live with him as his own son.

FRIENDS NEED TO BE AVAILABLE

One of the things that strengthens friendships is being available when we are needed. Sometimes our friends need us at a time that is inconvenient to us and we have to decide where our priorities are. I recall a time when I received a phone call telling me that a dear German friend named Brigitte, had been shot in the head five times by an intruder. At that time my schedule was not important. Being with her was the most important thing I could do. I flew to Sacramento and stayed in her home caring for her for a week. It was a scary time for both of us thinking the escaped intruder might return. Not only did she need my help but she needed a friend. That was 28 years ago and we are still good friends.

Another time a close friend named Dona was recuperating from lung cancer surgery so I flew to Salt Lake City to care for her. Although she was in a tremendous amount of pain, our time together was precious. I'm so glad I was able to spend that time with her because she passed away later that year. Before she died she sent me this Christmas poem she wrote.

A GIFT

What is a friend.... a good friend?
Someone who smiles with their eyes,
Listens with their heart,
Holds you by the hand.
Someone who calls you just to say
"I needed to hear your voice today."
Someone who is gentle and kind, and
Seems to know just what is on your mind.

What is a friend ... a good friend?
Someone to laugh with and cry with,
Someone you can talk to for hours
Without saying a word.
Someone who comforts you when you are sad, and
Puts a smile on your face.

What is a friend ... a good friend?
Someone who cares,
Someone who knows the true meaning of Christmas, and
Gives you the gift of LOVE.

By Dona Sparkman, 1987

Not only does the Bible speak about friendships, but famous writers down through the ages have written many things on the subject, such as:

"Thinking of friends and their worth is often enough to drive away an army of fears, regrets, and envies."

—William Shakespeare

"Friendships are gifts and expressions of God; they form when the divine spirit in one individual finds the divine spirit in another, and both deride

and cancel the thick walls of individual character, relation, age, sex and circumstance."

—Ralph Waldo Emerson

"We want to make sure we don't fall into the habit of walling friendships in or out."

—Robert Frost

Think about the friends who are important to you. Are you nurturing their friendship? If not, why not go out today and buy a couple of "Just thinking of you" cards and send to them. Years from now you may still have those friendships to treasure.

▼

CHAPTER 11

BLESSINGS GALORE!

Oh, give thanks to the LORD! Call upon His name; Make known His deeds among the peoples. Sing to Him, sing psalms to Him; Talk of all His wondrous works.

Psalm 105:1-22 (NKJ)

Do you wake up each morning saying, "Good morning, Lord."? Or do you say, "Oh, Lord, it's morning!"? Do you enjoy facing each new day? Do you feel like giving thanks for all the blessings God has given you? Most of us don't stop to consider how blessed we are. As a child I remember singing "Count your blessings, name them one by one; Count your many blessings see what God hath done." It was a hymn written by a man named Johnson Oatman, Jr. which has been sung in churches for decades. Many times in my older years the words of this song have come back to me as a reminder of how God has blessed my life. I must admit there were many days in my earlier years when I didn't greet each day with joy. As we mature spiritually we learn how to appreciate everything God does for us even when we're going through some hard times. We have to make a choice to say, "It's going to be a good day."

In the Bible there are many stories about women who God blessed in various ways. I think we can relate to the women I have chosen to write about even though they lived many years ago.

SARAH'S BLESSING

God blessed Sarah, Abraham's wife, with her first child, a son, at the age of ninety-one. Can you imagine that? I remember a time when I wanted desperately to get pregnant and I would cry every month when I had evidence that it hadn't happened. Finally after two years I conceived and I was elated. Sarah must have gone through many years of sadness because not only did she long to have a child of her own, but it was a disgrace for a woman to be barren. I can just imagine the joy that filled her heart when God told her husband that Sarah would conceive and have a son. She said, *"God has made me laugh, so that all who hear will laugh with me."* Genesis 21:6 (NKJ) Not only did God bless her with a child but He told Abraham that through this son he would be the father of many nations. Sarah was blessed indeed!

HANNAH'S BLESSING

In 1 Samuel, chapters 1 and 2, there is a story of another woman who could not bear children. Her name was Hannah. Hannah's husband had another wife named Penninah who had borne him several children and she would taunt Hannah. Penninah was jealous of Hannah because she was aware that their husband loved Hannah. Year after year this continued. One day when Hannah was crying, her husband asked her *"Why are you downhearted? Don't I mean more to you then ten sons?"* Obviously he didn't understand how much she longed to have a child of her own. Husbands are wonderful but they don't fill that need women have for a baby.

Hannah prayed to God and made a vow that if He would give her a son she would give him back to God. God honored her vow and blessed her with a son, Samuel, who she took to the temple to live as soon as he was weaned. Babies were weaned at about three years of age so to part with her precious three-year-old son must have been heart wrenching. But she had made a vow to God and she kept it. God later blessed her with five more children.

SHIRLEY'S BLESSING

Shirley is not a Bible character but she's my friend. She is counting her blessings because at the age of seventy-five she still has a job she loves. As a child Shirley took piano lessons for over seven years, but when she married right after high school she thought that would be the end of her piano playing so her mother sold her piano. Years later, at the age of fifty, after raising five daughters, she began to think about how much she used to enjoy playing the piano. While walking through WalMart one day she heard someone playing an organ which piqued her interest, so she decided to buy one. After taking the eight free lessons she enjoyed it so much she traded it for a larger one.

When she retired from her job she started working at a music store. They soon discovered that she played the organ and piano quite well and asked her to start teaching lessons. It wasn't long until she had thirty-two students. She continually bettered herself by taking advanced piano lessons. Before long she decided to start teaching in her own home to save the long drive to the music store, teaching both children and adults.

Shirley takes a personal interest in each of her students and thoroughly enjoys teaching them. She holds recitals in the living room of her home and serves punch and cookies in her lovely country kitchen. She feels very blessed to be doing something she loves and looks forward to many more years of teaching music.

BLESSINGS OF A CHRISTIAN FAMILY

Another blessing is having a Christian family. I was raised in a Christian home and all my siblings, children, and grandchildren have a relationship with Jesus. This is a rare thing today and I am so grateful. My heart aches for people who have unbelieving loved ones. It makes me count my blessings.

As a child all I wanted to be when I grew up was a wife and mother. I loved pretending my dolls were my children and knew someday I would have babies of my own. Since I had four brothers and no sisters I always hoped I would have girl babies. When I was twenty years old I had my first little girl, a beautiful red-haired baby named Deborah. Two years later God blessed me with another beautiful red-haired daughter; Barbara. They were the joy of my life. I had such fun dressing them with frilly little dresses and bonnets, they looked like a picture out of a magazine whenever I took them to church.

As the years passed and my girls weren't babies anymore, I longed for another baby to hold in my arms. God knew my heart's desire and blessed me with another beautiful red-haired baby girl; Rebecca. Despite her three-month colic she was a delight. It was like playing house as I did in my childhood. My dreams had come true.

Now those daughters have brought eight grandsons and one granddaughter into our family, as well as four great-grandchildren; two boys and two girls. One of the great-granddaughters is a carbon copy of my daughter, Deborah. The first time I saw her it took me back many years remembering Deborah as a child. Little Ashley looks and acts just like her. I guess that's a double blessing for me.

STEP SONS ARE A BLESSING

Having only daughters I was blessed when I married Jud to gain two step-sons, John and Mark. Although they had a wonderful mother whom they loved deeply until the day she died, they have lovingly accepted me into the family and I love them very much.

I also have a former step-son, Michael. When his father and I divorced he was only fourteen years old and I didn't realize the effect my leaving would have on him. He had felt abandoned by his natural mother because he lived with his father, and then I abandoned him also. I wasn't in touch with him for many years, but one day a few years ago I learned he was attending my brother's church in California and that he would like to see me. Michael could have resented me for not being there for him when he needed me, but when we got together he hugged me and said, "I love you." I didn't deserve that. I wept as he shared with me that he had been heavily addicted to drugs for fifteen years. He reminded me that I had taken him to a Billy Graham crusade and he had invited Jesus into his heart. All through his years of drug addiction He never felt that God left him and one day he recommitted his life to Jesus and was set free from his addiction instantly. Today he is a Pastor of Music in a church in California. I am so blessed that God has restored our relationship and even though we live far apart we keep in touch through e-mail and telephones.

NOT FEELING BLESSED?

Ladies, do you ever have a day when you don't feel at all blessed? You're just down in the dumps? We all have days like that. Here's a suggestion to help you get out of those "blues." Get a piece of paper and a pen and start writing down everything you can think of that God has blessed you with. Sometimes it's something as simple as "the sun is shining outside." Or maybe "I don't have to cook dinner tonight." or "My daughter called just to say hello." We really are more blessed than we realize. Counting our blessings is something we should do more often. The more we thank God for his blessings, the more He will bless us. *"It is wonderful to be alive! If a person lives to be very old, let him rejoice in every day of life, but let him remember that eternity is for longer; and that everything down here is futile in comparison.* Ecclesiastes 11:7-8 (Living)

CHAPTER 12

▼

BUILDING
YOUR LEGACY

At Epcot Center in Orlando, Florida right at the entrance there is a huge stone on which is engraved, "Leave a Legacy." Have you ever thought about the kind of legacy you are leaving for your family and friends? When President Reagan's son was asked what one word would best describe his father, his reply was "Integrity," Can you think of a word that would best describe you? I hope my children cannot remember what I was like when they were growing up. I was a screamer and spanker—not the gentle, tender-hearted person I'm trying to be in my older years. I'd like to think the changes God has made in me over the past twenty years will stand out in their memories. I want to leave a legacy of love that will go on long after I'm gone. While I'm still here I'm trying to be a living legacy letting them see the good things God has done and is still doing in my life. I want people to remember the way I care about hurting people, how I travel around speaking for women's groups sharing the love of Jesus, and how my desire to do God's will is the most important thing in my life. Letting others observe us as we live committed Christian lives is the best legacy we can leave. Ephesians 5:*15 Be very careful, then, how you live—not as unwise but as wise, making the most of every opportunity.* "(NIV)

Usually when we think of legacies we think of what our parents have passed on to us. What are some of the things you think of as legacies from your parents?

There are three things that my father passed down to me. I'm sure he never thought of them as legacies but perhaps they are. The first was his love for music. Daddy could play every wind instrument, piano, organ and accordion so I grew up surrounded by music. He encouraged each of us children to play musical instruments. He had accumulated an assortment of instruments, most of which were out of the ordinary. When I asked to play an instrument at the age of ten, instead of renting a clarinet he asked me to choose between an E Flat clarinet and a soprano saxophone, which he already owned. I chose the sax. In those days Kenny G had not made the soprano sax popular as it is today. It sounded sort of like a fish horn. When I took it to school I was kind of an odd ball but I played it in school bands and orchestras for the next seven years. Since my father was a Salvation Army Captain our musical family played on the street corners at Christmas time. When my father was asked to play a saxophone solo for our school assembly, much to my surprise he played something he had written titled "Esther." Needless to say, I was very proud.

The second thing my father passed down to me is his love for correct grammar. In addition to being a musician he was a linguist. He had a love for languages and taught himself Spanish, French and Italian which he could speak fluently. In addition he learned to read in a number of other languages. My youngest brother followed in his footsteps and learned to speak Spanish and Portugese. Although I enjoyed learning Spanish in high school, when I attempted to learn French at a college night school class, I quickly gave it up. Because of Daddy's love for languages he naturally wanted all of his children to learn good grammar, at least in English. I'm sure we didn't appreciate his constant correction of the way we spoke, but it has paid off and today all of us enjoy being able to speak correctly.

The third thing I'm not sure could be considered a legacy, but it's something my father enjoyed and I enjoy it also. It's moving to new places. I'm the only one out of five children who takes after him in this respect. Being in the Salvation Army is rather like being in the U.S. Army in that you move often. I lived in nine states before the age of eighteen, sometimes two or three different cities in one state. For some people this would have been traumatic, but I loved it. Daddy's genes, I guess. Every move for me was an adventure. I'm still like that. Jud and I have been married twenty-seven years and have moved thirteen times. My brothers who have hardly ever moved think I'm a little whacky to enjoy moving so much, but I love making new friends, fixing up a new home, and seeing new places. I tell them, "You spend money to go to nice places on vacations. We spend it on moving to new places."

MY MOTHER'S LEGACY

My mother was an outstanding seamstress and she loved to sew. I guess that is not a legacy in my case because I hate to sew. I'm sure this was a disappointment to my mother but she taught other people to sew so her legacy is still going on.

Mother was the most influential person in my life. I learned so many things by just being with her. She could make the dumpiest house into a warm, loving home. She could manage our home on a very meager income without complaining. She could never resist helping anyone in need. In the Salvation Army we met a lot of needy people. I remember one young woman who Mother brought home to live with us for a while. After a few days she disappeared taking with her the money from all our savings banks. Not all of the people she brought into our home were so ungrateful, however, and I'm sure many people have had good memories of Mother's kindness.

In the second chapter of II Kings there is a beautiful story of Elijah and Elisha. When God took Elijah up in a whirlwind into heaven Elisha picked up his mantel and when he struck the water with it, the waters parted so Elisha could cross over. The prophets who saw it knew that the spirit of Elijah had been passed on to Elisha. I had an experience about eighteen years ago that reminded me of this story.

My mother was a godly woman, and in my eyes, a tower of strength, so I was stunned when I learned that she had experienced a massive heart attack. The thought of losing her had never entered my mind. I was living in Lompoc, CA at the time, so I frantically drove the long drive to the Fountain Valley hospital praying all the way that she would not die. When I arrived at the hospital Mother was still alive, but in very serious condition. My brother informed me she had found a young woman she had befriended, lying in her driveway stoned on drugs. As she was dragging her into the house to put her into bed, the heart attack occurred. I was furious when I heard this and I blamed this girl for what happened to Mother.

When I was allowed to go into ICU Mother grabbed my hand and whispered, "Please don't blame her. It wasn't her fault. She needs someone to love her and she needs God. Please be kind to her." It annoyed me that Mother could always tell what I was thinking. I didn't even know this girl, but I hated her for causing Mother to have a heart attack. How could I be kind to her?

A few days later as I was in Mother's mobile home going through some papers on her desk to see if there were any bills that needed attention, I came across some letters dated nearly a year before. They were from people thanking Mother for all she had done to help them. One family had just moved here from Laos and despite a language barrier Mother had helped them find housing, and jobs. She also taught the wife how to sew on an American sewing machine so she could earn money. For some people Mother had made new clothes, for others she had taught them about Jesus and they had become Christians. As I read the letters I began to weep as I realized, "This is what Christianity is all about. Helping people."

For some time I had been urging Mother not to get so involved in other people's problems. "Take it easy, Mom, and enjoy your life." She was seventy-nine years old and I thought it was time she quit working so hard and start enjoying her life. I didn't realize that she was already enjoying her life. Material things or a life of leisure meant nothing to her. Helping people in need, telling them about Jesus; that's what brought her joy.

As I asked God to forgive me for being so blind and selfish, an unforgettable thing happened. I sensed God saying to me, "I gave your mother a love and compassion for people in need and now I am passing this on to you." I immediately recalled the story of Elijah and Elisha, so I understood what God was telling me. He was giving me my mother's mantle. I wept and asked God to forgive me for my hatred toward that young woman and for not understanding why Mother felt compelled to love and help people in need. A change took place in me at that moment that has altered the direction of my life forever. Mother went on to be with Jesus but she left me a beautiful legacy—a desire to help needy people. "*Those who live according to the sinful nature have their minds set on what that nature desires; but those who live in accordance with the Spirit have their minds set on what the Spirit desires.*" Romans 8:5 (NIV) This verse of scripture has become very meaningful to me since that day.

LEGACIES OF FAMOUS WOMEN

Monica, mother of Saint Augustine

In *Great Women of the Christian Faith*, I read about a woman who left a valuable legacy. Her name was Monica, the mother of Augustine. She prayed for her son eighteen years before God saved him from his evil ways. She also won over her husband and mother-in-law through her patience and humility. Monica inspired many great works of art and literature, and a painting of Augustine and Monica is still hanging in the National Gallery in London. Like Hannah, in the Bible, she consecrated her son to God before his birth. Augustine said she was God's handmaid who talked to him constantly about God, but none of it sank in until he was much older. In his autobiography, *Confessions,* he tells how God "drew his soul out of the profound darkness" because of his mother who wept on his behalf more than most mothers weep when their children die.

Madame Curie

A famous woman in our era was Madame Curie who became the first woman to receive a degree in physics at the Sorbonne in Paris She was one of only two women in a science program of more than 1000 men. She was first in her class and was the first woman to be appointed a professor at that institution. She was the first woman to win not one but two Nobel Prizes: the first for her contribution to the discovery of radioactivity and the second for her isolation of the elements polonium and radium. By the time she died she had become a legend and Paris streets are named after her, her face appears on the French 500 franc note as well as on stamps and coins. Think of what an inspiration her life was to other women to become achievers in what was thought to be "a man's world."

Mother Teresa

Mother Teresa has also left a legacy that has impacted the entire world. She knew from the age of twelve that she was called to be a missionary. She became a nun, a teacher, a missionary working in the sums of Calcutta where she started a school for slum children. She later started "The Missionaries of Charity", who cared for homeless people which became an international ministry. She died in 1997 but her name will never be forgotten. She said, "Like Jesus we belong to the world living not for ourselves but for others."

There were others who left great legacies as well: Vittoria Colonna who inspired Michelangelo by her great faith; Katherine Von Bora, wife of Martin Luther who has been described as the Proverbs 31 woman; Clara Swain, the first medical missionary, and great hymn writers like Fanny J. Crosby and Harriet Beecher Stowe. Think of the legacies these women left that have had a positive impact on our lives.

Rahab's Legacy

When we think of someone leaving a great legacy, most people wouldn't think about Rahab, whose story is in the book of Joshua. She was an Amorite, an idol worshipper, and a harlot. What kind of legacy could she possibly leave to anyone? I can't help but think she was an unhappy woman searching for God—the real God. She heard stories about what God had done for the Israelites and said to the spies, *"for the LORD your God, He is God in heaven above and on earth beneath."* She knew in her heart that they were serving the real God so she protected the spies Joshua sent into Jericho. She made a deal with them that when they conquered her city they would spare her life and that of her family. If she had been caught helping the spies she could have been put to death, but she was willing to take that chance to save her family. After the walls of Jericho miraculously crumbled and the Isrealites captured the city of Jericho, Rahab's families' lives were spared and God blessed her for her faith in Him. *"By faith the harlot Rahab did not perish with those who did not believe, when she had received the spies with peace."* Hebrews 11:31 (NKJ) Rahab married an Isrealite man and became an ancestress of Jesus. Down through the ages her story has been in the Bible for everyone to read. Quite a legacy!

LIVING LEGACIES

What have you learned that you can pass on to others. In the Living Bible in 2 Timothy 2:2 Paul writes to Timothy, *"For you must teach others those things you and many others have heard me speak about. Teach these great truths to trustworthy men who will, in turn, pass them on to others."* I recently read an article in the Kansas City Star about a sixty-five-year-old teacher who was retiring after forty-two years of teaching children with learning disabilities. I'm sure the parents of those children are grateful for the legacy this woman has planted into the lives of their children. This kind of legacy is never ending. If one child learns to read well and goes on to receive a good education, think of how many people could be touched by that one life. All because of one devoted teacher who wanted to open doors of opportunity for children with learning disabilities.

We don't have to be a teacher by profession to teach what we have learned. We can share our faith, our desire to please God, our values, our talents, and our exemplary character traits. I think of Florence and Marita Littauer who have spent their lives teaching women to become speakers and writers. Their legacy will go on through all the women who have sat under their teaching.

We may think that we have to be a parent in order to pass on a legacy, but that's not true. Whether you are a single person or a married person without children, you have the potential of influencing many lives. That is your legacy. Think of the people you have already influenced, whether in a negative way or a positive way. If it's negative you can start now to change that. You can become a godly example that will bless the lives of all your family and friends. Be a living legacy.

When I started writing this chapter I began to think about people my husband and I have influenced over the years and I realized that is a legacy from us. I'd like to share a few such stories with you.

A number of years ago a black man from Nigeria came to our church with his four young children ranging in ages from ten to fourteen. They were asked to sing for the congregation. While they were singing my heart went out to them. I just fell in love with these darling black children. My husband and I made a point of meeting their father after the service and we learned that although he had been in the United States for a number of years the children had just arrived. Their mother was not able to come because the government would not grant her a visa. The first thing we did was cook a big meal for them and deliver it to their house. Brisket, mashed potatoes, carrots, salad, rolls and a big triple chocolate cake. They were so appreciative and before we left their home the father asked the children to join hands with us and pray for us. I've never heard children that could pray like that. It was wonderful.

I gradually learned what kind of food they liked (carrots wasn't one of them) and would take them dinner occasionally. I invited the children to our home to teach them how to cook. Three of them were very interested and learned quickly. Whenever they had birthdays I baked them a birthday cake and we took them shopping to buy a birthday gift. In Nigeria they apparently did not celebrate birthdays until age sixteen, so they were thrilled. This went on for a few years, but then as the children grew older and we did not attend the same church any longer, we didn't see much of each other. We no longer live in the same city but I have fond memories of our times together and I believe Jud and I have passed on a legacy of love to them that has been a blessing in their lives.

Another story is about our grandson, Michael. We moved to Corpus Christi just after Michael was born. He was the first of my daughter, Becky's, four children. Like most grandparents we spent a lot of time with Michael and by the time he was two years old Jud decided to take one day a week and spend it with Michael so Becky and I could have some time together. He took Michael to many interesting places like the aquarium, the ships in the harbor, the draw bridge, a nursery, etc. We only lived in Corpus Christi four years but those two years Jud spent a day a week with Michael have made a lasting impression on him. Hopefully it is the kind of legacy Michael will pass on to his grandchildren. Michael's younger brother, Brandon, was only two years old when we moved away so he didn't get to have as much time with his grandpa as Michael did, but through the years Jud has shown all of Becky's children so much love they think he's a wonderful grandfather.

One day Jud was unable to take Michael so I filled in for him and I will always remember that day. I took Michael across a long bridge to Padre Island to a restaurant named Snoopy's. As we ate we could see all the boats passing by and Michael loved it. On the way home as we were driving across the bridge Michael said, "Meemaw, this is the best day of my life." For you grandmothers reading this, you can just imagine how that made me feel. I hope he'll always remember it.

Recently my oldest daughter, Debbe, told me she had sent a box containing everything for a birthday party to her young grandson. As she told me about it I remembered I had done the same thing years ago for her after she had left home. We don't realize how we influence our children by the things we do. It also brought to mind how I used to buy books for my grandchildren and read them aloud onto a cassette tape. That way when the children received the book they could hear it read in Grandma's voice. Now my daughter is considering doing that for her grandchildren. This can become a living legacy!

THE FAMILY TREE

Have you ever done a study of geneology to learn about your family tree? Most of us probably have not. But it's interesting to find out things about our ancestors to see if any of their lives have influenced ours. My first thoughts were about my grandparents. My mother's father was a doctor in Hayward, Wisconsin. I only got to be with him a couple of times when I was quite young but my mother told me many stories about how he cared so lovingly for people, many of whom could not pay for his services. I have a newspaper clipping about his death which I treasure because it tells how he told his family he saw angels coming to get him. He peacefully left this earth and went to his heavenly home while all his family stood watching.

My other grandfather was a Watkins salesman who never owned a car. Perhaps his walking made him a healthy person because the day he died at age ninety-six he had walked from his home to the downtown drugstore about a mile away. That's the way I want to live—healthy till the last day.

I never knew my mother's mother but I well remember Grandma Lena. She was an artist and an excellent cook. I take after her in these areas, plus I've been told I look a little like her. Many years ago Jud was working for an aerospace company and was sent to Cape Canaveral for three months. The company he worked for provided a furnished condo on the beach and I was able to go with him. Since he worked six or seven days a week I needed something to do so I decided to try my hand at painting. I was quite surprised to find out I had artistic talent. When we returned to California I pursued my interest in painting by taking some classes. I found that I could paint people quite well—much better than landscapes or still life—and I was very proud of some of the paintings I produced. However, every time I finished one I'd give it away. Consequently I have none of my paintings today. After about a year I became interested in teaching Bible and it took so much of my time I gave up painting and to this day have never painted another picture.

I remember going to Grandma Lena's home when she was eighty-seven and she cooked a fabulous meal. Fried chicken, mashed potatoes, some kind of vegetable and the best apple pie I've ever tasted. I have always remembered that meal. I guess her love for cooking has been passed down to me. I started cooking at age ten. My mother would let me plan the meals and cook them during summer vacations, so when I got married I already knew how to cook. I have made cookbooks of some of my favorite recipes for family members and friends as gifts. Six years ago I became a vegetarian so cooking has taken on a new challenge for me, but I still love it.

IT'S NOT TOO LATE

As we get older if we don't feel we have accomplished the things we'd like to in our lives, it's easy to think, "I haven't done anything—I have no legacy to leave for anyone." That doesn't have to be the case. It's not too late to start. The Bible tells us in Psalm 91:16 "*With long life I will satisfy him, And show him My salvation.*" (NKJ) The word "salvation" has many meanings, one of which is "victory." If we're going to be blessed with a long life, it's encouraging to look forward to a victorious one. It's up to us what we do with the years we have left. If we spend them doing whatever God leads us to do, we will have a legacy to leave those who follow after us.

If you have no idea how to go about this, I would suggest you reread chapters one through six. Maya Angelou said, "I've learned that people will forget what you said, people will forget what you did, but people will never forget how you made them feel." All of us can make a difference in other people's lives if we care enough to try. Eleanor Roosevelt said "When you cease to make a contribution you begin to die." Ask yourself this question, "What can I do today to brighten someone's life?" That's a start. Take one day at a time and let God open doors for you to bless other people. That will be your legacy.

I hope this chapter has caused you to give some thought to how you can be a living legacy. A legacy is not built in a day—it takes years. For many years my life was not the living legacy it is today. But God is so good and He gives us the opportunity to erase the past and start building a legacy we can be proud of—one that our families and friends will respect and honor.

My prayer is that this book has been an encouragement to each of you, no matter where you are along life's journey. Whether you're young, middle-aged or older, God has a plan for your life. If you will let Him He will help enjoy every stage of life and you will be able to say with me, THE BEST IS NOW!

RECOMMENDED READING

Aging:
What We've Learned so Far by Lucinda Secrest McDowell
Looking Forward to the Rest of Your Life by Lorry Lutz
Help, Lord, I'm Having a Senior Moment by Karen O'Connor

Forgiveness:
Total Forgiveness by R. T. Kendall
The Wounded Heart by Dr. Dan B. Allender

Health:
Deadly Emotions by Dr. Don Colbert
Lifelong Health by Dr. Mary Ruth Swope

Inspiration:
You've Got What it Takes by Marita Littauer
Dare to Dream by Florence Littauer
100 Christian Women Who Changed the 20th Century by Helen Kooiman
Hosier
Secrets of the Vine by Bruce Wilkinson
Battlefield of the Mind by Joyce Meyer

Personalities:
Personality Plus, Personality Plus for Couples and *Personality Plus for Parents* by
Florence Littauer
Personality Tree by Florence Littauer
Personality Puzzle by Marita Littauer
Getting Along With Almost Anybody by Florence and Marita Littauer

YOUR PERSONALITY PROFILE

In each of the following rows of four words across, place an X in front of the one or two words that most often applies to you. Continue through all forty lines. If you are not sure which word "most applies," ask a spouse or a friend, and think of what your answer would have been when you were a child. Use the word definitions on the next for the most accurate results.

STRENGTHS

1	Adventurous	Adaptable	Animated	Analytical
2	Persistent	Playful	Persuasive	Peaceful
3	Submissive	Self-sacrificing	Sociable	Strong-willed
4	Considerate	Controlled	Competitive	Convincing
5	Refreshing	Respectful	Reserved	Resourceful
6	Satisfied	Sensitive	Self-reliant	Spirited
7	Planner	Patient	Positive	Promoter
8	Sure	Spontaneous	Scheduled	Shy
9	Orderly	Obliging	Outspoken	Optimistic
10	Friendly	Faithful	Funny	Forceful
11	Daring	Delightful	Diplomatic	Detailed
12	Cheerful	Consistent	Cultured	Confident

13	Idealistic	Independent	Inoffensive	Inspiring
14	Demonstrative	Decisive	Dry humor	Deep
15	Mediator	Musical	Mover	Mixes easily
16	Thoughtful	Tenacious	Talker	Tolerant
17	Listener	Loyal	Leader	Lively
18	Contented	Chief	Chartmaker	Cute
19	Perfectionist	Pleasant	Productive	Popular
20	Bouncy	Bold	Behaved	Balanced

WEAKNESSES

21	Blank	Bashful	Brassy	Bossy
22	Undisciplined	Unsympathetic	Unenthusiastic	Unforgiving
23	Reticent	Resentful	Resistant	Repetitious
24	Fussy	Fearful	Forgetful	Frank
25	Impatient	Insecure	Indecisive	Interrupts
26	Unpopular	Uninvolved	Unpredictable	Unaffectionate
27	Headstrong	Haphazard	Hard to please	Hesitant
28	Plain	Pessimistic	Proud	Permissive
29	Angered easily	Aimless	Argumentative	Alienated
30	Naive	Negative attitude	Nervy	Nonchalant
31	Worrier	Withdrawn	Workaholic	Wants credit
32	Too sensitive	Tactless	Timid	Talkative
33	Doubtful	Disorganized	Domineering	Depressed
34	Inconsistent	Introvert	Intolerant	Indifferent

35	Messy	Moody	Mumbles	Manipulative
36	Slow	Stubborn	Show-off	Skeptical
37	Loner	Lord over others	Lazy	Loud
38	Sluggish	Suspicious	Short-tempered	Scatterbrained
39	Revengeful	Restless	Reluctant	Rash
40	Compromising	Critical	Crafty	Changeable

WORD DEFINITIONS

STRENGTHS

1

Adventurous. One who will take on new and daring enterprises with a determination to master them.

Adaptable. Easily fits and is comfortable in any situation.

Animated. Full of life, lively use of hand, arm, and face gestures.

Analytical. Likes to examine the parts for their logical and proper relationships.

2

Persistent. Sees one project through to its completion before starting another.

Playful. Full of fun and good humor.

Persuasive. Convinces through logic and fact rather than charm or power.

Peaceful. Seems undisturbed and tranquil and retreats from any form of strife.

3

Submissive. Easily accepts any other's point of view or desire with little need to assert his own opinion.

Self-sacrificing. Willingly gives up his own personal being for the sake of, or to meet the needs of others.

Sociable. One who sees being with others as an opportunity to be cute and entertaining rather than as a challenge or business opportunity.

Strong-willed. Determined to have one's own way.

4

Considerate. Having regard for the needs and feelings of others.

Controlled. Has emotional feelings but rarely displays them.

Competitive. Turns every situation, happening, or game into a contest and always plays to win!

Convincing. Can win you over to anything through the sheer charm of his personality.

5

Refreshing. Renews and stimulates or makes others feel good.

Respectful. Treats others with deference, honor, and esteem.

Reserved. Self-restrained in expression of emotion or enthusiasm.

Resourceful. Able to act quickly and effectively in virtually all situations.

6

Satisfied. A person who easily accepts any circumstance or situation.

Sensitive. Intensively cares about others, and what happens.

Self-reliant. An independent person who can fully rely on his own capabilities, judgment, and resources.

Spirited. Full of life and excitement.

7

Planner. Prefers to work out a detailed arrangement beforehand, for the accomplishment of project or goal, and prefers involvement with the planning stages and the finished product rather than the carrying out of the task.

Patient. Unmoved by delay, remains calm and tolerant.

Positive. Knows it will turn out right if he's in charge.

Promoter. Urges or compels others to go along, join, or invest through the charm of his own personality.

8

Sure. Confident, rarely hesitates or wavers.

Spontaneous. Prefers all of life to be impulsive, unpremeditated activity, not restricted by plans.

Scheduled. Makes, and lives, according to a daily plan, dislikes his plan to be interrupted.

Shy. Quiet, doesn't easily instigate a conversation.

9
Orderly. Having a methodical, systematic arrangement of things.
Obliging. Accommodating. One who is quick to do it another's way.
Outspoken. Speaks frankly and without reserve.
Optimistic. Sunny disposition who convinces self and others that everything will turn out all right.

10
Friendly. A responder rather than an initiator, seldom starts a conversation.
Faithful. Consistently reliable, steadfast, loyal, and devoted sometimes beyond reason.
Funny. Sparkling sense of humor that can make virtually any story into an hilarious event.
Forceful. A commanding personality whom others would hesitate to take a stand against.

11
Daring. Willing to take risks; fearless, bold.
Delightful. A person who is upbeat and fun to be with.
Diplomatic. Deals with people tactfully, sensitively, and patiently.
Detailed. Does everything in proper order with a clear memory of all the things that happen.

12
Cheerful. Consistently in good spirits and promoting happiness in others.
Consistent. Stays emotionally on an even keel, responding as one might expect.
Cultured. One whose interests involve both intellectual and artistic pursuits, such as theatre, symphony, ballet.
Confident. Self-assured and certain of own ability and success.

13
Idealistic. Visualizes things in their perfect form, and has a need to measure up to that standard himself.
Independent. Self-sufficient, self-supporting, self-confident and seems to have little need of help.

Inoffensive. A person who never says or causes anything unpleasant or objectionable.

Inspiring. Encourages others to work, join, or be involved, and makes the whole thing fun.

14

Demonstrative. Openly expresses emotion, especially affection, and doesn't hesitate to touch others while speaking to them.

Decisive. A person with quick, conclusive, judgment-making ability.

Dry humor. Exhibits "dry wit," usually one-liners which can be sarcastic in nature.

Deep. Intense and often introspective with a distaste for surface conversation and pursuits.

15

Mediator. Consistently finds him- or herself in the role of reconciling differences in order to avoid conflict.

Musical. Participates in or has a deep appreciation for music, is committed to music as an art form, rather than the fun of performance.

Mover. Driven by a need to be productive, is a leader whom others follow, finds it difficult to sit still.

Mixes easily. Loves a party and can't wait to meet everyone in the room, never meets a stranger.

16

Thoughtful. A considerate person who remembers special occasions and is quick to make a kind gesture.

Tenacious. Holds on firmly, stubbornly, and won't let go until the goal is accomplished.

Talker. Constantly talking, generally telling funny stories and entertaining everyone around, feeling the need to fill the silence in order to make others comfortable.

Tolerant. Easily accepts the thoughts and ways of others without the need to disagree with or change them.

17

Listener. Always seems willing to hear what you have to say.

Loyal. Faithful to a person, ideal, or job, sometimes beyond reason.

Leader. A natural born director, who is driven to be in charge, and often finds it difficult to believe that anyone else can do the job as well.

Lively. Full of life, vigorous, energetic.

18

Contented. Easily satisfied with what he has, rarely envious.

Chief. Commands leadership and expects people to follow.

Chartmaker. Organizes life, tasks, and problem solving by making lists, forms or graphs.

Cute. Precious, adorable, center of attention.

19

Perfectionist. Places high standards on himself, and often on others, desiring that everything be in proper order at all times.

Pleasant. Easygoing, easy to be around, easy to talk with.

Productive. Must constantly be working or achieving, often finds it very difficult to rest.

Popular. Life of the party and therefore much desired as a party guest.

20

Bouncy. A bubbly, lively personality, full of energy.

Bold. Fearless, daring, forward, unafraid of risk.

Behaved. Consistently desires to conduct himself within the realm of what he feels is proper.

Balanced. Stable, middle of the road personality, not subject to sharp highs or lows.

WEAKNESSES

21

Blank. A person who shows little facial expression or emotion.

Bashful. Shrinks from getting attention, resulting from self-consciousness.

Brassy. Showy, flashy, comes on strong, too loud.

Bossy. Commanding, domineering, sometimes overbearing in adult relationships.

22

Undisciplined. A person whose lack of order permeates most every area of his life.

Unsympathetic. Finds it difficult to relate to the problems or hurts of others.

Unenthusiastic. Tends to not get excited, often feeling it won't work anyway.

Unforgiving. One who has difficulty forgiving or forgetting a hurt or injustice done to them, apt to hold onto a grudge.

23

Reticent. Unwilling or struggles against getting involved, especially when complex.

Resentful. Often holds ill feelings as a result of real or imagined offenses.

Resistant. Strives, works against, or hesitates to accept any other way but his own.

Repetitious. Retells stories and incidents to entertain you without realizing he has already told the story several times before, is constantly needing something to say.

24

Fussy. Insistent over petty matters or details, calling for a great attention to trivial details.

Fearful. Often experiences feelings of deep concern, apprehension or anxiousness.

Forgetful. Lack of memory which is usually tied to a lack of discipline and not bothering to mentally record things that aren't fun.

Frank. Straightforward, outspoken, and doesn't mind telling you exactly what he thinks.

25

Impatient. A person who finds it difficult to endure irritation or wait for others.

Insecure. One who is apprehensive or lacks confidence.

Indecisive. The person who finds it difficult to make any decision at all. (Not the personality that labors long over each decision in order to make the perfect one.)

Interrupts. A person who is more of a talker than a listener, who starts speaking without even realizing someone else is already speaking.

26

Unpopular. A person whose intensity and demand for perfection can push others away.

Uninvolved. Has no desire to listen or become interested in clubs, groups, activities, or other people's lives.

Unpredictable. May be ecstatic one moment and down the next, or willing to help but then disappears, or promises to come but forgets to show up.

Unaffectionate. Finds it difficult to verbally or physically demonstrate tenderness openly.

27

Headstrong. Insists on having his own way.

Haphazard. Has no consistent way of doing things.

Hard to please. A person whose standards are set so high that it is difficult to ever satisfy them.

Hesitant. Slow to get moving and hard to get involved.

28

Plain. A middle-of-the-road personality without highs or lows and showing little, if any, emotion.

Pessimistic. While hoping for the best, this person generally sees the down side of a situation first.

Proud. One with great self-esteem who sees himself as always right and the best person for the job.

Permissive. Allows others (including children) to do as they please in order to keep from being disliked.

29

Angered easily. One who has a childlike flash-in-the-pan temper that expresses itself in tantrum style and is over and forgotten almost instantly.

Aimless. Not a goal-setter with little desire to be one.

Argumentative. Incites arguments generally because he is right no matter what the situation may be.

Alienated. Easily feels estranged from others, often because of insecurity or fear that others don't really enjoy his company.

30

Naive. Simple and child-like perspective, lacking sophistication or comprehension of what the deeper levels of life are really about.

Negative attitude. One whose attitude is seldom positive and is often able to see only the down or dark side of each situation.

Nervy. Full of confidence, fortitude, and sheer guts, often in a negative sense.

Nonchalant. Easy-going, unconcerned, indifferent.

31

Worrier. Consistently feels uncertain, troubled, or anxious.

Withdrawn. A person who pulls back to himself and needs a great deal of alone or isolation time.

Workaholic. An aggressive goal-setter who must be constantly productive and feels very guilty when resting, is not driven by a need for perfection or completion but by a need for accomplishment and reward.

Wants credit. Thrives on the credit or approval of others. As an entertainer this person feeds on the applause, laughter, and/or acceptance of an audience.

32

Too sensitive. Overly introspective and easily offended when misunderstood.

Tactless. Sometimes expresses himself in a somewhat offensive and inconsiderate way.

Timid. Shrinks from difficult situations.

Talkative. An entertaining, compulsive talker who finds it difficult to listen.

33

Doubtful. Characterized by uncertainty and lack of confidence that it will ever work out.

Disorganized. Lack of ability to ever get life in order.

Domineering. Compulsively takes control of situations and/or people, usually telling others what to do.

Depressed. A person who feels down much of the time.

34

Inconsistent. Erratic, contradictory, with actions and emotions not based on logic.

Introvert. A person whose thoughts and interest are directed inward, lives within himself.

Intolerant. Appears unable to withstand or accept another's attitudes, point of view or way of doing things.

Indifferent. A person to whom most things don't matter one way or the other.

35

Messy. Living in a state of disorder, unable to find things.

Moody. Doesn't get very high emotionally, but easily slips into low lows, often when feeling unappreciated.

Mumbles. Will talk quietly under the breath when pushed, doesn't bother to speak clearly.

Manipulative. Influences or manages shrewdly or deviously for his own advantage, will get his way somehow.

36

Slow. Doesn't often act or think quickly, too much of a bother.

Stubborn. Determined to exert his or her own will, not easily persuaded, obstinate.

Show-off. Needs to be the center of attention, wants to be watched.

Skeptical. Disbelieving, questioning the motive behind the words.

37

Loner. Requires a lot of private time and tends to avoid other people.

Lord over. Doesn't hesitate to let you know that he is right or is in control.

Lazy. Evaluates work or activity in terms of how much energy it will take.

Loud. A person whose laugh or voice can be heard above others in the room.

38

Sluggish. Slow to get started, needs push to be motivated.

Suspicious. Tends to suspect or distrust others or ideas.

Short-tempered. Has a demanding impatience-based anger and a short fuse. Anger is expressed when others are not moving fast enough or have not completed what they have been asked to do.

Scatterbrained. Lacks the power of concentration, or attention, flighty.

39

Revengeful. Knowingly or otherwise holds a grudge and punishes the offender, often by subtly withholding friendship or affection.

Restless. Likes constant new activity because it isn't fun to do the same things all the time.

Reluctant. Unwilling or struggles against getting involved.

Rash. May act hastily, without thinking things through, generally because of impatience.

40

Compromising. Will often relax his position, even when right, in order to avoid conflict.

Critical. Constantly evaluating and making judgments, frequently thinking or expressing negative reactions.

Crafty. Shrewd, one who can always find a way to get to the desired end.

Changeable. A child-like, short attention span that needs a lot of change and variety to keep from getting bored.

PERSONALITY
SCORING SHEET

Now transfer all your X's to the corresponding words on the Personality Scoring Sheet, and addup your totals. For example, if you checked Animated on the profile, check it on the scoring sheet. (Note: The words are in a different order on the profile and the scoring sheet.)

Strengths

	Popular Sanguine	Powerful Choleric	Perfect Melancholy	Peaceful Phlegmatic
1	Animated	Adventurous	Analytical	Adaptable
2	Playful	Persuasive	Persistent	Peaceful
3	Sociable	Strong-willed	Self-sacrificing	Submissive
4	Convincing	Competitive	Considerate	Controlled
5	Refreshing	Resourceful	Respectful	Reserved
6	Spirited	Self-reliant	Sensitive	Satisfied
7	Promoter	Positive	Planner	Patient
8	Spontaneous	Sure	Scheduled	Shy
9	Optimistic	Outspoken	Orderly	Obliging
10	Funny	Forceful	Faithful	Friendly

Strengths (Continued)

11	Delightful	Daring	Detailed	Diplomatic
12	Cheerful	Confident	Cultured	Consistent
13	Inspiring	Independent	Idealistic	Inoffensive
14	Demonstrative	Decisive	Deep	Dry humor
15	Mixes easily	Mover	Musical	Mediator
16	Talker	Tenacious	Thoughtful	Tolerant
17	Lively	Leader	Loyal	Listener
18	Cute	Chief	Chartmaker	Contented
19	Popular	Productive	Perfectionist	Pleasant
20	Bouncy	Bold	Behaved	Balanced

Totals
Strengths

Weaknesses

	Popular Sanguine	Powerful Choleric	Perfect Melancholy	Peaceful Phlegmatic
21	Brassy	Bossy	Bashful	Blank
22	Undisciplined	Unsympathetic	Unforgiving	Unenthusiastic
23	Repetitious	Resistant	Resentful	Reticent
24	Forgetful	Frank	Fussy	Fearful
25	Interrupts	Impatient	Insecure	Indecisive
26	Unpredictable	Unaffectionate	Unpopular	Uninvolved
27	Haphazard	Headstrong	Hard to please	Hesitant
28	Permissive	Proud	Pessimistic	Plain
29	Angered easily	Argumentative	Alienated	Aimless

Weaknesses (Continued)

30 Naive	Nervy	Negative attitude	Nonchalant
31 Wants credit	Workaholic	Withdrawn	Worrier
32 Talkative	Tactless	Too sensitive	Timid
33 Disorganized	Domineering	Depressed	Doubtful
34 Inconsistent	Intolerant	Introvert	Indifferent
35 Messy	Manipulative	Moody	Mumbles
36 Show-off	Stubborn	Skeptical	Slow
37 Loud	Lord over others	Loner	Lazy
38 Scatterbrained	Short-tempered	Suspicious	Sluggish
39 Restless	Rash	Revengeful	Reluctant
40 Changeable	Crafty	Critical	Compromising

Totals
Weaknesses

**Combined
Totals**

Once you've transferred your answers to the scoring sheet, added up your total number of answers in each of the four columns, and added your totals from both the strengths and weaknesses sections, you'll know your dominant personality type. You'll also know what combination you are. If, for example, your score is 35 in Powerful Choleric strengths and weaknesses, there's really little question. You're almost all Powerful Choleric. But if your score is, for example, 16 in Powerful Choleric, 14 in Perfect Melancholy, and 5 in each of the others, you're a

Powerful Choleric with a strong Perfect Melancholy. You'll also, of course, know your least dominant type.

A NOTE FROM THE AUTHOR

Thank you for letting me share with you parts of my life's journey. I pray it has been an encouragement to you in some way. Many of you may be able to relate to some of my experiences, so I want you to know that God can heal every kind of hurt. He can make you feel good about yourself and give you hope for your future. He can open doors of opportunity for you to do things that will not only make you feel fulfilled, but will be a blessing to others. He did all these things for me, so I know He would like to do them for you. He doesn't have favorites. He loves us all and wants the very best for our lives.

When we give ourselves to Christ and let Him be the Lord of our lives, He will make our lives beautiful beyond our wildest dreams. No matter where you are along your life's journey I hope you will be able to say with me, THE BEST IS NOW!

DISCUSSION QUESTIONS

I know that ladies enjoy getting together so perhaps you might like to have a group read this book and then get together to discuss it. Here are some questions for you to consider.

During your childhood did you feel loved? If so, who made you feel that way? What are some ways God has shown His love to you?

Have you discovered God's plan for your life? When and how did that happen? Have you ever experienced things in your life that were not part of God's plan for you? How have they affected your life?

Have you ever experienced a time when you were so busy doing "Christian" things you felt empty and dissatisfied inside? What did you do about it?

Do you feel confident that you are now part of God's family? Explain. Read John 1:12. Does that reassure you?

Have you ever felt that you are not pretty enough or talented enough to do something God has asked you to do? Read 1 Samuel 16:7.

What part of you is your soul? Do you find it difficult to relinquish control of your soul to God? Why? How does reading the Bible help you do this?

Why is it important to take good care of your body? What are some of the ways you have promoted a healthy body?

Have you ever heard God speak to you? How, when and where did it occur? Has it changed your life in any way?

What is one way to improve relationships? How should you treat other people in order to get along with them?

How does it make you feel when you are around an elderly person who is cranky and depressed? How can you avoid becoming this kind of person?

How important is it to have friends? What can you do to keep those friendships alive and well? Have you ever thought of Jesus as your friend? How can you develop a close relationship with Him?

Do you ever stop to consider how blessed you are? What are some of those blessings? Whenever you're feeling a little down, what is a good way to get over it and start feeling happy?

Have you ever thought about what people will say about you when you're gone? What kind of memories will people have about you? What are some of the traditions you passed on that people may want to continue?

How early in life can you start building legacies? Ephesians 5:15

978-0-595-45594-2
0-595-45594-8

Printed in the United States
83016LV00002B/103-165/A